3rd Workshop on Syntax and Structure in Statistical Translation 2009

(SSST-3)

Held at NAACL HLT 2009

Boulder, Colorado, USA
5 June 2009

Editors:

D. Wu **D. Chiang**

ISBN: 978-1-61738-570-4

Printed from e-media with permission by:

Curran Associates, Inc.
57 Morehouse Lane
Red Hook, NY 12571

Some format issues inherent in the e-media version may also appear in this print version.

Printed by Curran Associates, Inc. (2010)

For permission requests, please contact the Association for Computational Linguistics at the address below.

Association for Computational Linguistics
209 N. Eighth Street
Stroudsburg, Pennsylvania 18360

Phone: 1-570-476-8006
Fax: 1-570-476-0860

acl@aclweb.org

Additional copies of this publication are available from:

Curran Associates, Inc.
57 Morehouse Lane
Red Hook, NY 12571 USA
Phone: 845-758-0400
Fax: 845-758-2634
Email: curran@proceedings.com
Web: www.proceedings.com

Introduction

The Third Workshop on Syntax and Structure in Statistical Translation (SSST-3) was held on 5 June 2009 following the NAACL-HLT 2009 conference hosted by the University of Colorado at Boulder. Like the first two SSST workshops in 2007 and 2008, it aimed to bring together researchers from different communities working in the rapidly growing field of statistical, tree-structured models of natural language translation.

We were honored to have Alfred V. Aho deliver this year's invited keynote talk. Along with Lewis and Stearns' (1968) seminal "Syntax-directed transduction" introducing syntax-directed transduction grammars or SDTGs—to which synchronous CFGs are also equivalent—the classic pair of Aho and Ullman's (1969) articles "Syntax-directed translations and the pushdown assembler" and "Properties of syntax-directed translations" established the foundations of formal transduction approaches to translation. The motivation behind their formal language theory work was compiler translation of programming languages. But much of the current work at SSST reflects the evolution of those ideas into today's state-of-the-art approaches to modeling of syntax and structure in statistical machine translation of human languages.

Nowhere is it better demonstrated that research is healthily driven by the pollination of ideas across these disciplines. These formal language pioneers foresaw clearly the importance of formalizing compositional models of transduction. But without empirical research across various natural languages, formal language theorists would not perhaps have anticipated the wide applicability in human language translation of an intermediate restricted class of transductions between the syntax-directed transductions that can be described by SDTGs (or synchronous CFGs) at one extreme, and the very restricted finite-state transductions that can be described by FSTs at the other—like the broad equivalence class of inversion transductions that can be described by ITGs (which include synchronous/transduction grammars whose rules are all binary rank, ternary rank, or monotonically straight or inverted in reordering permutation). Nor might they have foreseen the success of the rich variety of statistical machine learning techniques that have been developed to induce such synchronous/transduction grammars, such as the techniques introduced by the hierarchical phrase-based translation approach. As has so often happened over the years of cross-fertilization cycles between formal language and natural language research, the theoretical and empirical lines of research provide mutual inspiration.

We selected ten papers for this year's workshop. Studies on alignment ranged from the theoretical (Søgaard) to data analysis (Nakazawa and Kurohashi; Søgaard and Kuhn; Jiang, Li, Yang and Zhao), to empirical impact on actual translation performance (Saers and Wu; Hashimoto, Yamamoto, Okuma, Sumita and Tokuda). New contributions to translation decoding included purely unsupervised methods leveraging compositional structure constraints (Saers and Wu), methods using explicit syntactic information (Chang, Tseng, Jurafsky and Manning; Khalilov, Fonollosa and Dras), as well as methods attempting to blend the two (Hashimoto, Yamamoto, Okuma, Sumita and Tokuda; Hanneman and Lavie). The program was rounded out by a paper considering the use of explicit syntax in automatic evaluation (Wang, Zhao, Yang and Li).

We would like to thank our authors and our Program Committee for making this year's SSST workshop another success.

Dekai Wu and David Chiang

Acknowledgements

This work was supported in part by the Defense Advanced Research Projects Agency (DARPA) under GALE Contract Nos. HR0011-06-C-0023, subcontract SRI International (Dekai Wu) and HR0011-06-C-0022, subcontract BBN Technologies 9500008412 (David Chiang). Any opinions, findings and conclusions or recommendations expressed in this material are those of the author(s) and do not necessarily reflect the views of the Defense Advanced Research Projects Agency.

Organizers:

Dekai Wu, Hong Kong University of Science and Technology (HKUST), Hong Kong
David Chiang, USC Information Sciences Institute, USA

Program Committee:

Srinivas Bangalore, AT&T Research, USA
Marine Carpuat, Hong Kong University of Science and Technology (HKUST), Hong Kong
Pascale Fung, Hong Kong University of Science and Technology (HKUST), Hong Kong
Daniel Gildea, University of Rochester, USA
Kevin Knight, USC Information Sciences Institute, USA
Jonas Kuhn, University of Potsdam, Germany
Yang Liu, Institute of Computing Technology, Chinese Academy of Sciences, China
Daniel Marcu, USC Information Sciences Institute, USA
Yuji Matsumoto, Nara Institute of Science and Technology, Japan
Hermann Ney, RWTH Aachen, Germany
Owen Rambow, Columbia University, USA
Philip Resnik, University of Maryland, USA
Stefan Riezler, Google Inc., USA
Libin Shen, BBN Technologies, USA
Christoph Tillmann, IBM T. J. Watson Research Center, USA
Stephan Vogel, Carnegie Mellon University, USA
Taro Watanabe, NTT Communication Science Laboratories, Japan
Andy Way, Dublin City University, Ireland
Yuk-Wah Wong, Google Inc., USA
Richard Zens, Google Inc., USA

Table of Contents

Conference Program

Friday, June 5, 2009

9:00–9:15 Opening

9:15–9:40 *Decoding with Syntactic and Non-Syntactic Phrases in a Syntax-Based Machine Translation System*
Greg HANNEMAN and Alon LAVIE

9:40–10:05 *Statistical Phrase Alignment Model Using Dependency Relation Probability*
Toshiaki NAKAZAWA and Sadao KUROHASHI

10:05–10:30 *Empirical Lower Bounds on Aligment Error Rates in Syntax-Based Machine Translation*
Anders SØGAARD and Jonas KUHN

10:30–11:00 Coffee Break

11:00–11:25 *Improving Phrase-Based Translation via Word Alignments from Stochastic Inversion Transduction Grammars*
Markus SAERS and Dekai WU

11:25–12:30 Invited Talk by Alfred V. AHO: "Unnatural Language Processing"

12:30–14:15 Lunch

14:15–14:40 *References Extension for the Automatic Evaluation of MT by Syntactic Hybridization*
Bo WANG, Tiejun ZHAO, Muyun YANG and Sheng LI

14:40–15:05 *A Study of Translation Rule Classification for Syntax-based Statistical Machine Translation*
Hongfei JIANG, Sheng LI, Muyun YANG and Tiejun ZHAO

15:05–15:30 *Discriminative Reordering with Chinese Grammatical Relations Features*
Pi-Chuan CHANG, Huihsin TSENG, Dan JURAFSKY and Christopher D. MANNING

15:30–16:00 Coffee Break

16:00–16:25 *On the Complexity of Alignment Problems in Two Synchronous Grammar Formalisms*
Anders SØGAARD

Friday, June 5, 2009 (continued)

16:25–16:50 *Reordering Model Using Syntactic Information of a Source Tree for Statistical Machine Translation*
Kei HASHIMOTO, Hirohumi YAMAMOTO, Hideo OKUMA, Eiichiro SUMITA and Keiichi TOKUDA

16:50–17:15 *Coupling Hierarchical Word Reordering and Decoding in Phrase-Based Statistical Machine Translation*
Maxim KHALILOV, José A. R. FONOLLOSA and Mark DRAS

17:15–17:30 Concluding Discussion

Decoding with Syntactic and Non-Syntactic Phrases in a Syntax-Based Machine Translation System

Greg Hanneman and **Alon Lavie**
Language Technologies Institute
Carnegie Mellon University
Pittsburgh, PA 15213 USA
{ghannema, alavie}@cs.cmu.edu

Abstract

A key concern in building syntax-based machine translation systems is how to improve coverage by incorporating more traditional phrase-based SMT phrase pairs that do not correspond to syntactic constituents. At the same time, it is desirable to include as much syntactic information in the system as possible in order to carry out linguistically motivated reordering, for example. We apply an extended and modified version of the approach of Tinsley et al. (2007), extracting syntax-based phrase pairs from a large parallel parsed corpus, combining them with PBSMT phrases, and performing joint decoding in a syntax-based MT framework without loss of translation quality. This effectively addresses the low coverage of purely syntactic MT without discarding syntactic information. Further, we show the potential for improved translation results with the inclusion of a syntactic grammar. We also introduce a new syntax-prioritized technique for combining syntactic and non-syntactic phrases that reduces overall phrase table size and decoding time by 61%, with only a minimal drop in automatic translation metric scores.

1 Introduction

The dominance of traditional phrase-based statistical machine translation (PBSMT) models (Koehn et al., 2003) has recently been challenged by the development and improvement of a number of new models that explicity take into account the syntax of the sentences being translated. One simple approach is to limit the phrases learned by a standard PBSMT translation model to only those contiguous sequences of words that additionally correspond to constituents in a syntactic parse tree. However, a total reliance on such syntax-based phrases has been shown to be detrimental to translation quality, as the space of phrase segmentation of a parallel sentence is heavily constrained by both the source-side and target-side tree structures. Noting that the number of phrase pairs extracted from a corpus is reduced by around 80% when they are required to correspond to syntactic constituents, Koehn et al. (2003) observed that many non-constituent phrase pairs that would not be included in a syntax-only model are in fact extremely important to system performance. Since then, researchers have explored effective ways for combining phrase pairs derived from syntax-aware methods with those extracted from more traditional PBSMT. Briefly stated, the goal is to retain the high level of coverage provided by non-syntactic PBSMT phrases while simultaneously incorporating and exploiting specific syntactic knowledge.

Zollmann and Venugopal (2006) overcome the restrictiveness of the syntax-only model by starting with a complete set of phrases as produced by traditional PBSMT heuristics, then annotating the target side of each phrasal entry with the label of the constituent node in the target-side parse tree that subsumes the span. They then introduce new constituent labels to handle the cases where the phrasal entries do not exactly correspond to the syntactic constituents. Liu et al. (2006) also add non-syntactic PBSMT phrases into their tree-to-string translation system. Working from the other direction, Marton and Resnik (2008) extend a hierarchical PBSMT

Proceedings of SSST-3, Third Workshop on Syntax and Structure in Statistical Translation, pages 1–9,
Boulder, Colorado, June 2009.

system with a number of features to prefer or disprefer certain types of syntactic phrases in different contexts. Restructuring the parse trees to ease their restrictiveness is another recent approach: in particular, Wang et al. (2007) binarize source-side parse trees in order to provide phrase pair coverage for phrases that are partially syntactic.

Tinsley et al. (2007) showed an improvement over a PBSMT baseline on four tasks in bidirectional German–English and Spanish–English translation by incorporating syntactic phrases derived from parallel trees into the PBSMT translation model. They first word align and extract phrases from a parallel corpus using the open-source Moses PBSMT toolkit (Koehn et al., 2007), which provides a baseline SMT system. Then, both sides of the parallel corpus are parsed with independent automatic parsers, subtrees from the resulting parallel treebank are aligned, and an additional set of phrases (with each phrase corresponding to a syntactic constituent in the parse tree) is extracted. The authors report statistically significant improvements in translation quality, as measured by a variety of automatic metrics, when the two types of phrases are combined in the Moses decoder.

Our approach in this paper is structurally similar to that of Tinsley et al. (2007), but we extend or modify it in a number of key ways. First, we extract both non-syntactic PBSMT and syntax-driven phrases from a parallel corpus that is two orders of magnitude larger, making our system competitive in size to state-of-the-art SMT systems elsewhere. Second, we apply a different algorithm for subtree alignment, proposed by Lavie et al. (2008), which proceeds bottom-up from existing statistical word alignments, rather than inducing them top-down from lexical alignment probabilities. Third, in addition to straightforwardly combining syntax-derived phrases with traditional PBSMT phrases, we demonstrate a new combination technique that removes PBSMT phrases whose source-language strings are already covered by a syntax-derived phrase. This new syntax-prioritized technique results in a 61% reduction in the size of the combined phrase table with only a minimal decrease in automatic translation metric scores. Finally, and crucially, we carry out the joint decoding over both syntactic and non-syntactic phrase pairs in a syntax-aware MT system, which allows a syntactic grammar to be put in place on top of the phrase pairs to carry out linguistically motivated reordering, hierarchical decoding, and other operations.

After this introduction, we first describe the base MT system we used, its formalism for specifying translation rules, and the method for extracting syntax-derived phrase pairs from a parallel corpus (Section 2). Section 3 gives the two methods for combining PBSMT phrases with our syntactic phrases, and introduces our first steps with including a grammar in the syntax-based translation framework. The results of our experiments are described in Section 4 and are further discussed in Section 5. Finally, Section 6 offers some conclusions and directions for future work.

2 Base Translation System

The base MT system used for our experiments is the statistical transfer ("Stat-XFER") framework (Lavie, 2008). The core of the framework is a transfer engine using two language-pair-dependent resources: a grammar of weighted synchronous context-free rules, and a probabilistic bilingual lexicon. Once the resources have been provided, the Stat-XFER framework carries out translation in a two-stage process, first applying the lexicon and grammar to synchronously parse an input sentence, then running a monotonic decoder over the resulting lattice of scored translation pieces assembled during parsing to produce a final string output. Reordering is applied only in the first stage, driven by the syntactic grammar; the second-stage monotonic decoder only assembles translation fragments into complete hypotheses.

2.1 Lexicon and Grammar Formalism

Each Stat-XFER bilingual lexicon entry has a synchronous context-free grammar (SCFG) expression of the source- and target-language production rules, shown in abbreviated format below, where c_s and c_t represent source- and target-side syntactic category labels and w_s and w_t represent source- and target-side word or phrase strings.

$$c_s :: c_t \rightarrow [w_s] :: [w_t]$$

Each entry in the lexicon is assigned a pair of rule scores ($r_{t|s}$ and $r_{s|t}$) based on c_s, w_s, c_t, and w_t[1]. The $r_{t|s}$ score is a maximum-likelihood estimate of the distribution of target-language translations and source- and target-language syntactic categories given the source string (Equation 1); this is similar to the usual "target-given-source" phrasal probability in standard SMT systems. The $r_{s|t}$ score is similar, but calculated in the reverse direction to give a source-given-target probability (Equation 2).

$$r_{t|s} = \frac{\#(w_t, c_t, w_s, c_s)}{\#(w_s) + 1} \quad (1)$$

$$r_{s|t} = \frac{\#(w_t, c_t, w_s, c_s)}{\#(w_t) + 1} \quad (2)$$

The add-one smoothing in the denominators counteracts overestimation of the rule scores of lexical entries with very infrequent source or target sides.

Stat-XFER grammar rules have a similar form, shown below via an example.

$$\text{NP} :: \text{NP} \rightarrow [\text{DET}^1\ \text{N}^2\ de\ \text{N}^3] :: [\text{DET}^1\ \text{N}^3\ \text{N}^2]$$

The SCFG backbone may include lexicalized items, as above, as well as non-terminals and pre-terminals from the grammar. Constituent alignment information, shown here as co-indexes on the non-terminals, specifies one-to-one correspondences between source-language and target-language constituents on the right-hand side of the SCFG rule. Rule scores $r_{t|s}$ and $r_{s|t}$ for grammar rules, if they are learned from data, are calculated in the same way as the scores for lexical entries.

2.2 Syntax-Based Phrase Extraction

In this section, we briefly summarize the automatic resource extraction approach described by Lavie et al. (2008) and recently extended by Ambati and Lavie (2008), which we use here, specifically as applied to the extraction of syntax-based phrase pairs for the bilingual lexicon.

The grammar and lexicon are extracted from a large parallel corpus that has been statistically word-aligned and independently parsed on both sides with automatic parsers. Word-level entries for the bilingual lexicon are directly taken from the word alignments; corresponding syntactic categories for the left-hand side of the SCFG rules are obtained from the preterminal nodes of the parse trees. Phrase-level entries for the lexicon are based on node-to-node alignments in the parallel parse trees. In the straightforward "tree-to-tree" scenario, a given node n_s in one parse tree S will be aligned to a node n_t in the other parse tree T if the words in the yield of n_s are all either aligned to words within the yield of n_t or have no alignment at all. If there are multiple nodes n_t satisfying this constraint, the node in the tree closest to the leaves is selected. Each aligned node pair (n_s, n_t) produces a phrase-level entry in the lexicon, where the left-hand sides of the SCFG rule are the labels of n_s and n_t, and the right-hand sides are the yields of those two nodes in their respective trees. In the expanded "tree-to-tree-string" configuration, if no suitable node n_t exists, a new node n'_s is introduced into T as a projection of n_s, spanning the yield of the words in T aligned to the yield of n_s. At the end of the extraction process in either case, the entry counts are collected and scored in the manner described in Section 2.1.

3 Combination with PBSMT Phrases

Conceptually, we take the opposite approach to that of Tinsley et al. (2007) by adding traditional PBSMT phrases into a syntax-based MT system rather than the other way around. We begin by running steps 3 through 5 of the Moses training script (Koehn et al., 2007)[2], which results in a list of phrase pair instances for the same word-aligned corpus to which we applied the syntax-based extraction methods in Section 2.2. Given the two sets of phrases, we explore two methods of combining them.

- **Direct Combination.** Following the method of Tinsley et al. (2007), we directly combine the counts of observed syntax-based phrase pairs with the counts of observed PBSMT phrase pairs. This results in a modified probability model in which a higher likelihood is moved onto syntactic phrase pairs that were also extractable using traditional PBSMT heuristics. It

[1]If no syntactic category information is available, c_s and c_t can be set to dummy values, but the rule score equations remain unchanged.

[2]See also www.statmt.org/moses.

Decoder	Phrase Type	# Phrases	METEOR	BLEU	TER
Stat-XFER	Syntactic only, PHR	917,266	0.5654	0.2734	56.49
Stat-XFER	Syntactic only, frag	1,081,233	0.5653	0.2741	56.54
Stat-XFER	Syntactic only, gra	1,081,233	0.5665	0.2772	56.26
Stat-XFER	PBSMT only	8,069,480	0.5835	**0.3018**	54.26
Stat-XFER	Direct combination, PHR	8,071,773	0.5835	**0.3009**	54.21
Stat-XFER	Direct combination, frag	9,150,713	0.5841	**0.3026**	54.52
Stat-XFER	Direct combination, gra	9,150,713	0.5855	**0.3034**	54.28
Stat-XFER	Syntax-prioritized, PHR	2,888,154	0.5800	0.2961	54.79
Stat-XFER	Syntax-prioritized, frag	3,052,121	0.5802	0.2979	54.78
Stat-XFER	Syntax-prioritized, gra	3,052,121	0.5813	0.2991	54.73
Moses	PBSMT only, mono	8,145,083	0.5911	0.3139	53.77
Moses	PBSMT only, lex RO	8,145,083	0.5940	0.3190	53.48

Figure 1: Results on the test set for all phrase table configurations. For BLEU, bold type indicates the best Stat-XFER baseline and the configurations statistically equivalent to it (paired bootstrap resampling with $n = 1000$, $p = 0.05$).

also allows either extraction mechanism to introduce new entries into the combined phrase table that were not extracted by the other, thus permitting the system to take full advantage of complementary information provided by PBSMT phrases that do not correspond to syntactic constituents.

- **Syntax-Prioritized Combination.** Under this method, we take advantage of the fact that syntax-based phrase pairs are likely to be more precise translational equivalences than traditional PBSMT phrase pairs, since constituent boundaries are taken into account during phrase extraction. PBSMT phrases whose source-side strings are already covered by an entry from the syntactic phrase table are removed; the remaining PBSMT phrases are combined as in the direct combination method above. The effect on the overall system is to trust the syntactic phrase pairs in the cases where they exist, supplementing with PBSMT phrase pairs for non-constituents.

For each type of phrase-pair combination, we test three variants when jointly decoding syntax-based phrases, which come with syntactic information, along with PBSMT phrases, which do not. In the first configuration ("PHR"), all extracted phrase labels for syntactic phrases are mapped to a generic "PHR" tag to simulate standard SMT monotonic decoding; this matches the treatment given throughout to our extracted non-syntactic phrases. In the second variant ("frag"), the phrase labels in the large nonterminal sets used by our source- and target-side parsers are mapped down to a smaller set of 19 labels that we use for both sides. The same translation phrase pair may occur with multiple category labels in this case if it was extracted with different syntactic categories from different trees in the corpus. In a third variant ("gra"), a small manually developed grammar is additionally inserted into the system. The Stat-XFER system behaves the same way in each variant. All phrase pairs are applied jointly to the input sentence during the parsing stage, getting added to the translation according to their syntactic category and scores, although phrases tagged as PHR cannot participate in any grammar rules. The second-stage decoder then receives the joint lattice and assembles complete output hypotheses regardless of syntactic category labels.

4 Experiments

We extracted the lexical resources for our MT system from version 3 of the French–English Europarl parallel corpus (Koehn, 2005), using the officially released training set from the 2008 Workshop in Statistical Machine Translation (WMT)[3]. This gives us a corpus of approximately 1.2 million sentence

[3]www.statmt.org/wmt08/shared-task.html

Phrase Table	# Entries	# Source Sides	Amb. Factor
Total syntax-prioritized table	3,052,121	113,988	26.8
Syntactic component	1,081,233	39,105	27.7
PBSMT component	1,970,888	74,883	26.3
Total baseline PBSMT table	8,069,480	113,972	70.8
Overlap with syntax-prioritized	6,098,592	39,089	156.0

Figure 2: Statistical characteristics of the syntax-prioritized phrase table (top) compared with the baseline PBSMT phrase table (bottom). The ambiguity factor is the ratio of the number of unique entries to the number of unique source sides, or the average number of target-language alternatives per source phrase.

pairs. Statistical word alignments are learned in both directions with GIZA++ (Och and Ney, 2003), then combined with the "grow-diag-final" heuristic. For the extraction of syntax-based phrase pairs, we obtain English-side constituency parses using the Stanford parser (Klein and Manning, 2003), and French-side constituency parses using the Xerox XIP parser (Aït-Mokhtar et al., 2001). In phrase extraction, we concentrate on the expanded tree-to-tree-string scenario described in Section 2.2, as it results in a nearly 50% increase in the number of extracted phrase pairs over the tree-to-tree method. For decoding, we construct a suffix-array language model (Zhang and Vogel, 2006) from a corpus of 430 million words, including the English side of our training data, the English side of the Hansard corpus, and newswire data. The "gra" variant uses a nine-rule grammar that is meant to address the most common low-level reorderings between French and English, focusing mainly on the reordering between nouns or noun phrases and adjectives or adjective phrases.

Our test set is the 2000-sentence "test2007" data set, also released as part of the WMT workshop series. We report case-insensitive scores on version 0.6 of METEOR (Lavie and Agarwal, 2007) with all modules enabled, version 1.04 of IBM-style BLEU (Papineni et al., 2002), and version 5 of TER (Snover et al., 2006).

Figure 1 gives an overall summary of our results on the test2007 data. Overall, we train and test 10 different configurations of phrase pairs in the Stat-XFER decoder. We begin by testing each type of phrase separately, producing one set of baseline systems with only phrase pairs that correspond to syntactic constituents ("Syntactic only") and one baseline system with only phrase pairs that were extracted from Moses ("PBSMT only"). We then test our two combination techniques, and their variants, as described in Section 3. Statistical significance is tested on the BLEU metric using paired bootstrap resampling (Koehn, 2004) with $n = 1000$ and $p = 0.05$. In the figure, the best baseline system and the configurations statistically equivalent to it are indicated in bold type. In addition to automatic metric scores, we also list the number of unique phrase pairs extracted for each configuration. (Because of the large number of phrase pairs, we pre-filter them to only the set whose source sides appear in the test data; these numbers are the ones reported.)

As an additional point of comparison, we build and tune a Moses MT system on the same data as our Stat-XFER experiments. The Moses system with a 4-gram language model and a distance-6 lexical reordering model ("lex RO") scores similarly to state-of-the-art systems of this type on the test2007 French–English data (Callison-Burch et al., 2007). Without the reordering model ("mono"), the Moses system is as comparable as possible in design and resources to the Stat-XFER PBSMT-only configuration. We do not propose in this paper a head-to-head performance comparison between the Stat-XFER and Moses decoders; rather, we report results on both to gain a better understanding of the impact of the non-syntactic lexical reordering model in Moses compared with the impact of the syntactic grammar in Stat-XFER.

5 Discussion

5.1 Phrasal Coverage and Precision

One observation apparent in Figure 1 is that we have again confirmed that a total restriction to syntax-

Source:	Il faut que l' opinion publique soit informée pleinement sur les caractéristiques du test dont je parle .
Reference:	Public opinion must be fully informed of the characteristics of the test I am talking about .
Syntax only:	It | is | that | the public | be informed | fully | on | the characteristics | of the test | I am talking about | .
PBSMT only:	We must | that public opinion gets noticed | fully | on the characteristics of the | test | above .
Direct comb.:	We must | that public opinion gets noticed | fully on | the characteristics of the | test | above .
Syntax-prioritized:	It is important that | *the public* | *be informed* | fully on | *the characteristics* | *of the test* | *I am talking about* | .

Figure 3: A translation example from the test set showing the output's division into phrases. In the syntax-prioritized translation, English phrases that derived from syntax-based phrasal entries are shown in italics.

based phrases is detrimental to output quality. A likely reason for this, as Tinsley et al. (2007) suggested, is that the improved precision and informativeness of the syntactic phrases is not enough to overcome their relative scarcity when compared to non-syntactic PBSMT phrases. (The syntactic phrase table is only 11 to 13% of the size of the PBSMT phrase table.) It is important to note that this scarcity occurs at the *phrasal* level: though there are 294 unknown word types in our test set when translating with only syntactic phrase pairs, this number only drops to 277 with the inclusion of PBSMT phrases. The largest phrase table configuration, direct combination, yields statistically equivalent performance to the baseline system created using standard PBSMT extraction heuristics. Its key benefit is that the inclusion of syntactic information in the phrase pairs, where possible, leaves open the door to further improvement in scores with the addition of a larger syntactic grammar. We have thus addressed the syntax-only phrase coverage problem without giving up syntactic information.

An interesting conclusion is revealed in the analysis of the sizes and relative overlaps of the phrase tables in each of our translation conditions. In the absence of significant grammar, the equivalence of scores between the PBSMT-only and direct-combination scenarios is understandable given the minimal change in the size of the phrase table. Out of nearly 8.1 million entries, only 2293 entirely new entries are provided by adding the syntactic phrase table; further, these phrases are relatively rare long phrases that do not have much effect on the translation of the overall test set. On the other hand, the syntax-prioritized phrase table is extremely different in nature — and only 37.8% of the size of the baseline PBSMT phrase table — yet still attains nearly the same automatic metric scores. There, we can clearly see the effect of the syntactic phrases, since the 3,052,121 phrases used in the fragmented variant of that scenario are more noticibly split between 1,970,888 PBSMT phrases (64.6%) and 1,081,233 syntax-based phrases (35.4%).

Some statistics for the makeup of the syntax-prioritized phrase table, compared to the baseline PBSMT phrase table, are shown in Figure 2. For each, we calculate the "ambiguity factor," or the average number of target-language alternatives for each source-language phrase in the table. This analysis shows not only that the distribution of traditional PBSMT phrases is rather different from that of the syntactic phrases, it is also different from the non-syntactic PBSMT phrases that are preserved in the syntax-prioritized table. In effect, given a baseline PBSMT phrase table, the syntax prioritization replaces phrase entries for 39,089 source-language phrases, each with an average of 156 different target-language translations, with 39,105 source phrases, each with an average of 27.7 syntactically motivated target translations — a net savings of 5.0 million

Source: Je veux saluer , à mon tour , l' intervention forte et substantielle du président Prodi .
Reference: I too would like to welcome Mr Prodi 's forceful and meaningful intervention .

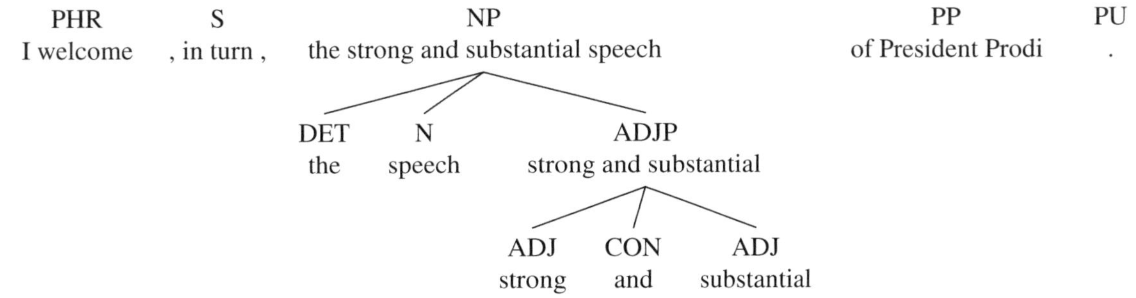

Figure 4: A translation example from the test set showing the result of including the nine-rule grammar in the syntax-prioritized combination. The SMT-only translation of the noun phrase is *the decisive intervention and substantial.*

phrase pairs. This is a strong indication that, because of the more accurate phrase boundary detection, the syntactic phrases are a much more precise representation of translational equivalence. An additional benefit is a significant reduction in decoding time, from an average of 27.3 seconds per sentence with the baseline PBSMT phrase table to 10.7 seconds per sentence with the syntax-prioritized table with the grammar included.

Improved precision due to the inclusion of syntactic phrases can be seen by examining a translation example and the phrasal chunks that produce it (Figure 3). In the syntax-prioritized output, the English phrases deriving from syntax-based phrase pairs are shown in italic, while the phrases deriving from PBSMT pairs are in normal type. The example shows an effective combination of on-target translations for syntactic constituents, when they are available, with non-syntactic phrases to handle constituent boundaries or places where parallel constituents are difficult to extract. The translation pieces *be informed* and *I am talking about*, though they exist in the baseline PBSMT phrase table, do not make it into the top-best translation in the PBSMT-only scenario because of its high ambiguity factor.

5.2 Effect of Syntactic Information

Although our current experiments do not show a significant increase in automatic metric scores with the addition of a small grammar, we can see the potential power of grammar in examining further sentences from the output. For example, in Figure 4, standard PBSMT phrase extraction is able to pick up the adjective–noun reordering when translating from *intervention forte* to *decisive intervention.* However, in this sentence we have an adjective *phrase* following the noun, and there is no pre-extracted phrase pair for the entire constituent, so our system built from only PBSMT phrases produces the incorrect noun phrase translation *the decisive intervention and substantial.* Our nine-rule grammar, specifically targeted for this scenario, is able to correct the structure of the sentence by applying two rules to produce *the strong and substantial speech.*

Analysis of the entire test set further suggests that even our small grammar produces correct and precise output across all phrase table configurations, although the total number of applications of the nine rules remains low. There are 590 rule applications in the one-best output on the test set in the syntax-only configuration, 472 applications in the syntax-prioritized configuration, and 216 applications in the direct combination. In each configuration, we manually inspected all rule applications in the first 200 sentences and classified them as correctly reordering words in the English output ("good"), incorrectly reordering ("bad"), or "null." This last category denotes applications of monotonic structure-building rules that did not feed into a higher-level reordering rule. The results of this analysis are shown in Figure 5. Overall, we find that the grammar is 97% accurate in its applications, making helpful reordering changes 88% of the time.

Given the preceding analysis — and the fact that our inclusion of a lexicalized reordering model in

Phrase Table	Good	Bad	Null
Syntactic only	47	3	8
Syntax-prioritized	45	1	3
Direct combination	25	0	0

Figure 5: Manual analysis of grammar rule applications in the first 200 sentences of the test set.

Moses resulted in automatic metric gains of only 0.0051 BLEU, 0.0029 METEOR, and 0.29 TER — we believe that further experiments with a much larger syntactic grammar will lead to a more significant improvement in automatic metric scores and translation quality.

6 Conclusions and Future Work

We have extended and applied an algorithm for combining syntax-based phrases from a parallel parsed corpus with non-syntactic phrases from phrase-based SMT within the context of a statistical syntax-based translation framework. Using a much larger corpus than has previously been employed for this approach, we produce jointly decoded output statistically equivalent to a monotonic decoding using standard PBSMT phrase-extraction heuristics, retaining syntactic information and setting the stage for further improvements by incorporating a syntactic grammar into the translation framework. Our preliminary nine-rule grammar, targeted for two specific English–French linguistic phenomena, already shows promise in performing linguistically motivated reordering that cannot be captured formally by a standard PBSMT model.

We present a syntax-prioritized method of combining phrase types into a single phrase table by always selecting a syntax-based phrase pair when one is available for a given source string. This new combination style reduces the size of the resulting phrase table and total decoding time by 61%, with only a minor degradation in MT performance. We suggest that this is because the syntax-derived phrases, when they can be extracted, are a much more precise method of describing correct translational equivalences.

As yet, we have made only minimal use of the Stat-XFER framework's grammar capabilities. In our experiments, the full tree-to-tree-string rule-extraction process of Ambati and Lavie (2008) produces more than 2 million unique SCFG rules when applied to a corpus the size of the Europarl. Not only is translating with such a large set computationally intractable, but empirically nearly 90% of the rules were observed only once in the parallel parsed corpus, making it difficult to separate rare but correct rules from those due to noise in the parses and word alignments. With the view of moving beyond our manually written nine-rule grammar, but wanting to get only the most useful rules from the entire automatically extracted set, we are currently investigating methods for automatic scoring or selection of a reasonable number of grammar rules for a particular language pair. Given that the majority of our phrase pairs, even in the syntax-prioritized combination, are non-syntactic, we have also conducted preliminary experiments with "syntactifying" them so that they may also be used by grammar rules to produce larger translation fragments.

The experiments in this paper used the grow-diag-final heuristic for word alignment combination because it has been shown to provide the highest precision on the subtree node alignment method by which we extract syntax-based phrase pairs (Lavie et al., 2008). However, this is a trade-off that sacrifices some amount of recall. Experimenting with different symmetric alignment heuristics may lead to a more optimal configuration for phrase-pair extraction or combination with PBSMT phrases. We also suspect that the choice of source- and target-side parsers plays a significant role in the number and nature of phrase pairs we extract; to address this, we are in the process of re-trying our line of experiments using the Berkeley parser (Petrov and Klein, 2007) for English, French, or both.

Acknowledgments

This research was supported in part by NSF grant IIS-0534217 (LETRAS) and the DARPA GALE program. We thank the members of the Parsing and Semantics group at Xerox Research Center Europe for parsing the French data with their XIP parser.

References

Salah Aït-Mokhtar, Jean-Pierre Chanod, and Claude Roux. 2001. A multi-input dependency parser. In

Proceedings of the Seventh International Workshop on Parsing Technologies, Beijing, China, October.

Vamshi Ambati and Alon Lavie. 2008. Improving syntax driven translation models by re-structuring divergent and non-isomorphic parse tree structures. In *Proceedings of the Eighth Conference of the Association for Machine Translation in the Americas*, pages 235–244, Waikiki, HI, October.

Chris Callison-Burch, Cameron Fordyce, Philipp Koehn, Christof Monz, and Josh Schroeder. 2007. (Meta-) evaluation of machine translation. In *Proceedings of the Second Workshop on Statistical Machine Translation*, pages 136–158, Prague, Czech Republic, June.

Dan Klein and Christopher D. Manning. 2003. Fast exact inference with a factored model for natural language parsing. In *Advances in Neural Information Processing Systems 15*, pages 3–10. MIT Press, Cambridge, MA.

Philipp Koehn, Franz Josef Och, and Daniel Marcu. 2003. Statistical phrase-based translation. In *Proceedings of HLT-NAACL 2003*, pages 48–54, Edmonton, Alberta, May–June.

Philipp Koehn, Hieu Hoang, Alexandra Birch, Chris Callison-Burch, Marcello Federico, Nicola Bertoldi, Brooke Cowan, Wade Shen, Christine Moran, Richard Zens, Chris Dyer, Ondrej Bojar, Alexandra Constantin, and Evan Herbst. 2007. Moses: Open source toolkit for statistical machine translation. In *Proceedings of the ACL 2007 Demo and Poster Sessions*, pages 177–180, Prague, Czech Republic, June.

Philipp Koehn. 2004. Statistical significance tests for machine translation evaluation. In *Proceedings of EMNLP 2004*, pages 388–395, Barcelona, Spain, July.

Philipp Koehn. 2005. Europarl: A parallel corpus for statistical machine translation. In *Proceedings of the 10th Machine Translation Summit*, pages 79–86, Phuket, Thailand, September.

Alon Lavie and Abhaya Agarwal. 2007. METEOR: An automatic metric for MT evaluation with high levels of correlation with human judgments. In *Proceedings of the Second Workshop on Statistical Machine Translation*, pages 228–231, Prague, Czech Republic, June.

Alon Lavie, Alok Parlikar, and Vamshi Ambati. 2008. Syntax-driven learning of sub-sentential translation equivalents and translation rules from parsed parallel corpora. In *Proceedings of the Second ACL Workshop on Syntax and Structure in Statistical Translation*, pages 87–95, Columbus, OH, June.

Alon Lavie. 2008. Stat-XFER: A general search-based syntax-driven framework for machine translation. In *Computational Linguistics and Intelligent Text Processing*, Lecture Notes in Computer Science, pages 362–375. Springer.

Yang Liu, Qun Liu, and Shouxun Lin. 2006. Tree-to-string alignment template for statistical machine translation. In *Proceedings of the 21st International Conference on Computational Linguistics and 44th Annual Meeting of the ACL*, pages 609–616, Sydney, Australia, July.

Yuval Marton and Philip Resnik. 2008. Soft syntactic constraints for hierarchical phrase-based translation. In *Proceedings of ACL-08: HLT*, pages 1003–1011, Columbus, OH, June.

Franz Josef Och and Hermann Ney. 2003. A systematic comparison of various statistical alignment models. *Computational Linguistics*, 29(1):19–51.

Kishore Papineni, Salim Roukos, Todd Ward, and Wei-Jing Zhu. 2002. BLEU: A method for automatic evalution of machine translation. In *Proceedings of the 40th Annual Meeting of the Association for Computational Linguistics*, pages 311–318, Philadelphia, PA, July.

Slav Petrov and Dan Klein. 2007. Improved inference for unlexicalized parsing. In *Proceedings of NAACL HLT 2007*, pages 404–411, Rochester, NY, April.

Matthew Snover, Bonnie Dorr, Richard Schwartz, Linnea Micciulla, and John Makhoul. 2006. A study of translation edit rate with targeted human annotation. In *Proceedings of the Seventh Conference of the Association for Machine Translation in the Americas*, pages 223–231, Cambridge, MA, August.

John Tinsley, Mary Hearne, and Andy Way. 2007. Exploiting parallel treebanks to improve phrase-based statistical machine translation. In *Proceedings of the Sixth International Workshop on Treebanks and Linguistic Theories*, pages 175–187, Bergen, Norway, December.

Wei Wang, Kevin Knight, and Daniel Marcu. 2007. Binarizing syntax trees to improve syntax-based machine translation accuracy. In *Proceedings of the 2007 Joint Conference on Empirical Methods in Natural Language Processing and Computational Natural Language Learning*, pages 746–754, Prague, Czech Republic, June.

Ying Zhang and Stephan Vogel. 2006. Suffix array and its applications in empirical natural language processing. Technical Report CMU-LTI-06-010, Carnegie Mellon University, Pittsburgh, PA, December.

Andreas Zollmann and Ashish Venugopal. 2006. Syntax augmented machine translation via chart parsing. In *Proceedings of the Workshop on Statistical Machine Translation*, pages 138–141, New York, NY, June.

Statistical Phrase Alignment Model Using Dependency Relation Probability

Toshiaki Nakazawa **Sadao Kurohashi**

Graduate School of Informatics, Kyoto University
Yoshida-honmachi, Sakyo-ku
Kyoto, 606-8501, Japan
nakazawa@nlp.kuee.kyoto-u.ac.jp kuro@i.kyoto-u.ac.jp

Abstract

When aligning very different language pairs, the most important needs are the use of structural information and the capability of generating one-to-many or many-to-many correspondences. In this paper, we propose a novel phrase alignment method which models word or phrase dependency relations in dependency tree structures of source and target languages. The dependency relation model is a kind of tree-based reordering model, and can handle non-local reorderings which sequential word-based models often cannot handle properly. The model is also capable of estimating phrase correspondences automatically without any heuristic rules. Experimental results of alignment show that our model could achieve F-measure 1.7 points higher than the conventional word alignment model with symmetrization algorithms.

1 Introduction

We consider that there are two important needs in aligning parallel sentences written in very different languages such as Japanese and English. One is to adopt structural or dependency analysis into the alignment process to overcome the difference in word order. The other is that the method needs to have the capability of generating phrase correspondences, that is, one-to-many or many-to-many word correspondences. Most existing alignment methods simply consider a sentence as a sequence of words (Brown et al., 1993), and generate phrase correspondences using heuristic rules (Koehn et al., 2003). Some studies incorporate structural information into the alignment process *after* this simple word alignment (Quirk et al., 2005; Cowan et al., 2006). However, this is not sufficient because the basic word alignment itself is not good.

On the other hand, a few models have been proposed which use structural information from the beginning of the alignment process. Watanabe et al. (2000) and Menezes and Richardson (2001) proposed a structural alignment methods. These methods use heuristic rules when resolving correspondence ambiguities. Yamada and Knight (2001) and Gildea (2003) proposed a tree-based probabilistic alignment methods. These methods reorder, insert or delete sub-trees on one side to reproduce the other side, but the constraints of using syntactic information is often too rigid. Yamada and Knight flattened the trees by collapsing nodes. Gildea cloned sub-trees to deal with the problem. Cherry and Lin (2003) proposed a model which uses a source side dependency tree structure and constructs a discriminative model. However, there is the defect that its alignment unit is a word, so it can only find one-to-one alignments. Nakazawa and Kurohashi (2008) also proposed a model focusing on the dependency relations. Their model has the constraint that content words can only correspond to content words on the other side, and the same applies for function words. This sometimes leads to an incorrect alignment. We have removed this constraint to make more flexible alignments possible. Moreover, in their model, some function words are brought together, and thus they cannot handle the situation where each function word corresponds to a different part. The smallest unit of our model is a single word, which should solve this problem.

Proceedings of SSST-3, Third Workshop on Syntax and Structure in Statistical Translation, pages 10–18,
Boulder, Colorado, June 2009.

In this paper, we propose a novel phrase alignment method which models word or phrase dependency relations in dependency tree structures of source and target languages. For a pair of correspondences which has a parent-child relation on one side, the dependency relation on the other side is defined as the relation between the two correspondences. It is a kind of tree-based reordering model, and can capture non-local reorderings which sequential word-based models often cannot handle properly. The model is also capable of estimating phrase correspondences automatically without heuristic rules. The model is trained in two steps: Step 1 estimates word translation probabilities, and Step 2 estimates phrase translation probabilities and dependency relation probabilities. Both Step 1 and Step 2 are performed iteratively by the EM algorithm. During the Step 2 iterations, word correspondences are grown into phrase correspondences.

2 Proposed Model

We suppose that Japanese is the source language and English is the target language in the description of our model. Note that the model is not specialized for this language pair, and it can be applied to any language pair.

Because our model uses dependency tree structures, both source and target sentences are parsed beforehand. Japanese sentences are converted into dependency structures using the morphological analyzer JUMAN (Kurohashi et al., 1994), and the dependency analyzer KNP (Kawahara and Kurohashi, 2006). MSTparser (McDonald et al., 2005) is used to convert English sentences. Figure 1 shows an example of dependency structures. The root of a tree is placed at the extreme left and words are placed from top to bottom.

2.1 Overview

This section outlines our proposed model in comparison to the IBM models, which are the conventional statistical alignment models.

In the IBM models (Brown et al., 1993), the best alignment $\hat{\mathbf{a}}$ between a given source sentence $\mathbf{f}$ and its target sentence $\mathbf{e}$ is acquired by the following equation:

$$\begin{aligned}\hat{\mathbf{a}} &= \operatorname*{argmax}_{\mathbf{a}} p(\mathbf{f}, \mathbf{a}|\mathbf{e}) \\ &= \operatorname*{argmax}_{\mathbf{a}} p(\mathbf{f}|\mathbf{e}, \mathbf{a}) \cdot p(\mathbf{a}|\mathbf{e}) \qquad (1)\end{aligned}$$

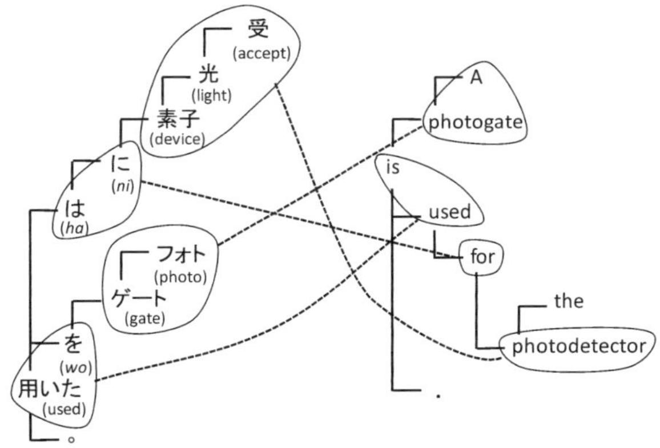

Figure 1: An example of a dependency tree and its alignment.

where $p(\mathbf{f}|\mathbf{e}, \mathbf{a})$ is called *lexicon probability* and $p(\mathbf{a}|\mathbf{e})$ is called *alignment probability*.

Suppose $\mathbf{f}$ consists of n words $f_1, f_2, ..., f_n$, and $\mathbf{e}$ consists of m words $e_1, e_2, ..., e_m$ and a NULL word (e_0). The alignment mapping $\mathbf{a}$ consists of associations $j \rightarrow i = a_j$ from source position j to target position $i = a_j$. The two probabilities above are broken down as:

$$p(\mathbf{f}|\mathbf{e}, \mathbf{a}) = \prod_{j=1}^{J} p(f_j|e_{a_j}) \qquad (2)$$

$$p(\mathbf{a}|\mathbf{e}) = \prod_{i=1}^{I} p(\Delta j|e_i) \qquad (3)$$

where Δj is a relative position of words in the source side which corresponds to e_i. Equation 2 is the product of the word translation probabilities, and Equation 3 is the product of relative position probabilities.

In the proposed model, we refine the IBM models in three ways. First, as for Equation 2, we consider phrases instead of words. Second, as for Equation 3, we consider dependencies of words instead of their positions in a sentence.

Finally, the proposed model can find the best alignment $\hat{\mathbf{a}}$ by not using $\mathbf{f}$-to-$\mathbf{e}$ alone, but simultaneously with $\mathbf{e}$-to-$\mathbf{f}$. That is, Equation 1 is modified as follows:

$$\begin{aligned}\hat{\mathbf{a}} = \operatorname*{argmax}_{\mathbf{a}} \quad & p(\mathbf{f}|\mathbf{e}, \mathbf{a}) \cdot p(\mathbf{a}|\mathbf{e}) \cdot \\ & p(\mathbf{e}|\mathbf{f}, \mathbf{a}) \cdot p(\mathbf{a}|\mathbf{f}) \qquad (4)\end{aligned}$$

Since our model regards a phrase as a basic unit, the above formula is calculated in a straightforward way. In contrast, the IBM models can consider a many-to-one alignment by combining one-to-one alignments, but they cannot consider a one-to-many or many-to-many alignment.

The models are estimated by EM-like algorithm which is very similar to (Liang et al., 2006). The important difference is that we are using tree structures.

We maximize the data likelihood:

$$\max_{\theta_{ef},\theta_{fe}} \sum_{\mathbf{f},\mathbf{e}} (\log p_{ef}(\mathbf{f},\mathbf{e};\theta_{ef}) + \log p_{fe}(\mathbf{f},\mathbf{e};\theta_{fe})) \tag{5}$$

In the E-step, we compute the posterior distribution of the alignments with the current parameter θ:

$$q(\mathbf{a};\mathbf{f},\mathbf{e}) := p_{ef}(\mathbf{a}|\mathbf{f},\mathbf{e};\theta_{ef}) \cdot p_{fe}(\mathbf{a}|\mathbf{f},\mathbf{e};\theta_{fe}) \tag{6}$$

In the M-step, we update the parameter θ:

$$\begin{aligned}\theta' := &\operatorname*{argmax}_{\theta} \sum_{\mathbf{a},\mathbf{f},\mathbf{e}} q(\mathbf{a};\mathbf{f},\mathbf{e}) \log p_{ef}(\mathbf{a},\mathbf{f},\mathbf{e};\theta_{ef}) \\ &+ \sum_{\mathbf{a},\mathbf{f},\mathbf{e}} q(\mathbf{a};\mathbf{f},\mathbf{e}) \log p_{fe}(\mathbf{a},\mathbf{f},\mathbf{e};\theta_{fe}) \\ = &\operatorname*{argmax}_{\theta} \sum_{\mathbf{a},\mathbf{f},\mathbf{e}} q(\mathbf{a};\mathbf{f},\mathbf{e}) \log p(\mathbf{e}) \cdot p_{ef}(\mathbf{a},\mathbf{f}|\mathbf{e};\theta_{ef}) \\ &+ \sum_{\mathbf{a},\mathbf{f},\mathbf{e}} q(\mathbf{a};\mathbf{f},\mathbf{e}) \log p(\mathbf{f}) \cdot p_{fe}(\mathbf{a},\mathbf{e}|\mathbf{f};\theta_{fe})\end{aligned} \tag{7}$$

Note that $p(\mathbf{e})$ and $p(\mathbf{f})$ have no effect on maximization, and $p_{ef}(\mathbf{a},\mathbf{f}|\mathbf{e};\theta_{ef})$ and $p_{fe}(\mathbf{a},\mathbf{e}|\mathbf{f};\theta_{fe})$ appeared in Equation 1 or Equation 4.

In the following sections, we decompose the lexicon probability and alignment probability.

2.2 Phrase Translation Probability

Suppose $\mathbf{f}$ consists of N phrases $F_1, F_2, ..., F_N$, and $\mathbf{e}$ consists of M phrases $E_1, E_2, ..., E_M$. The alignment mapping $\mathbf{a}$ consists of associations $j \to i = A_j$ from source phrase j to target phrase $i = A_j$.

We consider *phrase translation probability* $p(F_j|E_i)$ instead of word translation probability. There is one restriction: that phrases composed of more than one word cannot be aligned to NULL. Only a single word can be aligned to NULL.

We denote a phrase which the word f_j belongs to as $F_{s(j)}$, and a phrase which the word e_i belongs to as $E_{t(i)}$. With these notations, we refine Equation 2 as follows:

$$p(\mathbf{f}|\mathbf{e},\mathbf{a}) = \prod_{j=1}^{J} p(F_{s(j)}|E_{A_{s(j)}}) \tag{8}$$

Suppose phrase F_j and E_i are aligned where the number of words in F_j is denoted by $|F_j|$ and that number in E_i is $|E_i|$, the probability mass related to this alignment in Equation 8 is as follows:

$$p(F_j|E_i)^{|F_j|} \cdot p(E_i|F_j)^{|E_i|} \tag{9}$$

We call this probability for the link between F_j and E_i *phrase alignment probability*. The upper part of Table 1 shows phrase alignment probabilities for the alignment in Figure 1.

2.3 Dependency Relation Probability

The reordering model in the IBM Models is defined on the relative position between an alignment and its previous alignment, as shown in Equation 3. Our model, on the other hand, considers dependencies of words instead of positional relations.

We start with a dependency relation where f_c depends on f_p in the source sentence. In a possible alignment, f_c belongs to $F_{s(c)}$, f_p belongs to $F_{s(p)}$, and $F_{s(c)}$ depends on $F_{s(p)}$. In this situation, we consider the relation between $E_{A_{s(p)}}$ and $E_{A_{s(c)}}$. Even if two languages have different word order, their dependency structures are similar in many cases, and $E_{A_{s(c)}}$ tends to depend on $E_{A_{s(p)}}$. Our model takes this tendency into consideration. In order to denote the relationship between phrases, we introduce $rel(E_{A_{s(p)}}, E_{A_{s(c)}})$. This is defined as the path from $E_{A_{s(p)}}$ to $E_{A_{s(c)}}$. It is represented by applying the notations below:

- 'c' if going down to the *c*hild node
- 'p' if going down to the *p*arent node

For example, in Figure 1, the path from "for" to "photodetector" is 'c', from "the" to "for" is 'p;p' because it travels across two nodes. All the phrases are considered as a single node, so the path from "photogate" to "the" is 'p;c;c;c' with the alignment in Figure 1.

We refine Equation 3 using rel as follows:

$$p(\mathbf{a}|\mathbf{e}) = \prod_{(p,c)\in D_{s\text{-}pc}} p_t(rel(E_{A_{s(p)}}, E_{A_{s(c)}})|\text{pc}) \tag{10}$$

where $D_{s\text{-}pc}$ denotes a set of parent-child word pairs in the source sentence. We call $p_t(rel(E_{A_{s(p)}}, E_{A_{s(c)}})|\text{pc})$ target side *dependency relation probability*. p_t is a kind of tree-based reordering model.

Table 1: A probability calculation example.

Source	Target	Phrase alignment probability
受光素子	photodetector	$p($受光素子$\|\text{photodetector})^3 \cdot p(\text{photodetector}\|$受光素子$)$
には	for	$p($には$\|\text{for})^2 \cdot p(\text{for}\|$には$)$
フォトゲート	photogate	$p($フォトゲート$\|\text{a photogate})^2 \cdot p(\text{a photogate}\|$フォトゲート$)^2$
を用いた	is used	$p($を用いた$\|\text{is used})^2 \cdot p(\text{is used}\|$を用いた$)^2$
NULL	the	$p(\text{the}\|\text{NULL})$

Source		Target dependency relation probability
c	p	
受	光	$p_t(\text{SAME}\|\text{pc})$
光	素子	$p_t(\text{SAME}\|\text{pc})$
素子	に	$p_t(\text{c}\|\text{pc})$
に	は	$p_t(\text{SAME}\|\text{pc})$
は	用いた	$p_t(\text{c}\|\text{pc})$
フォト	ゲート	$p_t(\text{SAME}\|\text{pc})$
ゲート	を	$p_t(\text{c}\|\text{pc})$
を	用いた	$p_t(\text{SAME}\|\text{pc})$

Target		Source dependency relation probability
c	p	
A	photogate	$p_s(\text{SAME}\|\text{pc})$
photogate	is	$p_s(\text{c}\|\text{pc})$
used	is	$p_s(\text{SAME}\|\text{pc})$
for	used	$p_s(\text{c}\|\text{pc})$
the	photodetector	$p_s(\text{NULL\_c}\|\text{pc})$
photodetector	for	$p_s(\text{c}\|\text{pc})$

There are some special cases for rel. When $F_{s(c)}$ and $F_{s(p)}$ are the same, that is, f_c and f_p belong to the same phrase, rel is represented as 'SAME'. When f_p is aligned to NULL, f_c is aligned to NULL, and both of them are aligned to NULL, rel is represented as 'NULL_p', 'NULL_c', and 'NULL_b', respectively. The lower part of Table 1 shows dependency relation probabilities corresponding to Figure 1.

Actually, we extend the dependency relation probability to consider a wider relation, i.e, the grandparent-child relation, as follows:

$$p(\mathbf{a}|\mathbf{e}) = \prod_{(p,c)\in D_{s\text{-}pc}} p_t(rel(E_{A_{s(p)}}, E_{A_{s(c)}})|\text{pc}) \cdot \prod_{(g,c)\in D_{s\text{-}gc}} p_t(rel(E_{A_{s(g)}}, E_{A_{s(c)}})|\text{gc}) \quad (11)$$

where $D_{s\text{-}gc}$ denotes a set of grandparent-child word pairs in the source sentence.

3 Model Training

Our model is trained in two steps. In Step 1, word translation probability is estimated. Then, in Step 2, possible phrases are acquired, and both phrase translation probability and dependency relation probability are estimated. In both steps, parameter estimation is done with the EM algorithm.

3.1 Step 1

In Step 1, word translation probability in each direction is estimated independently. This is done in exactly the same way as in IBM Model 1.

In this process, the alignment unit is a word. When we consider **f**-to-**e** alignment, each word on the source side f_j can correspond to a word on the target side e_i or a NULL word, independently of other source words. The probability of one possible alignment $\mathbf{a}$ is calculated as follows:

$$p(\mathbf{a}, \mathbf{f}|\mathbf{e}) = \prod_{j=1}^{J} p(f_j|e_{a_j}) \quad (12)$$

By considering all possible alignments, $p(\mathbf{f}|\mathbf{e})$ is calculated as:

$$p(\mathbf{f}|\mathbf{e}) = \sum_{\mathbf{a}} p(\mathbf{a}, \mathbf{f}|\mathbf{e}) \quad (13)$$

As initial parameters of $p(f|e)$, we use uniform probabilities. Then, after calculating Equation 12 and 13, we give the fractional count $\frac{p(\mathbf{a},\mathbf{f}|\mathbf{e})}{p(\mathbf{f}|\mathbf{e})}$ to all word alignments in $\mathbf{a}$, and we estimate $p(f|e)$ by MLE. We perform this estimation iteratively.

The inverse model **e**-to-**f** can be calculated in the same manner.

3.2 Step 2

Both phrase translation probability and dependency relation probability are estimated, and one undirected alignment is found using the **e**-to-**f** and **f**-to-**e** probabilities simultaneously in this step. In contrast to Step 1, it is impossible to enumerate all the possible alignments. To find the best alignment, we first create an initial alignment based on phrase translation probability only, and then gradually revise it by considering the dependency relation probability with a hill-climbing algorithm.

The initial parameters of Step 2 are calculated as follows. The dependency relation probability is calculated using the final alignment result of Step 1, and we use the word translation probability estimated in Step 1 as the initial phrase translation probability.

3.2.1 Initial Alignment

We first create an initial alignment based on the phrase translation probability without considering the dependency relation probabilities.

For all the combinations of possible phrases (including NULL), phrase alignment probabilities are calculated (equation 9). Correspondences are adopted one by one in descending order of geometric mean of the phrase alignment probabilities. All the words should be aligned only once, that is, the correspondences are adopted exclusively. Generation of possible phrases is explained in Section 3.2.3.

3.2.2 Hill-climbing

To find better alignments, the initial alignment is gradually revised with a hill-climbing algorithm. We use four kinds of revising operations:

Swap: Focusing on any two correspondences, the partners are swapped. In the first step in Figure2, the correspondences "光 $\leftrightarrow$ photogate" and "フォト ゲート $\leftrightarrow$ photodetector" are swapped to "光 $\leftrightarrow$ photodetector" and "フォト ゲート $\leftrightarrow$ photogate".

Extend: Focusing on one correspondence, the source or target phrase is extended to include its neighboring (parent or child) NULL-aligned word.

Add: A new correspondence is added between a source word and a target word both of which are aligned to NULL.

Reject: A correspondence is rejected and the source and target phrase are aligned to NULL.

Figure 2 shows an illustrative example of hill climbing. The alignment is revised only if the alignment probability gets increased. It is repeated until no operation can improve the alignment probability, and the final state is the best approximate alignment. As a by-product of hill-climbing, pseudo n-best alignment can be acquired. It is used in collecting fractional counts.

3.2.3 Phrase Generation

If there is a word which is aligned to NULL in the best approximate alignment, a new possible phrase is generated by merging the word into a neighboring phrase which is not aligned to NULL. In the last alignment result in Figure 2, for example, "素子" is treated as being included in the correspondence between "受 光" and "photodetector" and the correspondence between "に" and "for". As a result, we consider the correspondence between "受 光 素子" and "photodetector" and the correspondence between "素子 に" and "for" existing in parallel sentences. The new possible phrase is taken into consideration from the next iteration.

3.2.4 Model Estimation

Collecting all the alignment results, we estimate phrase alignment probabilities and dependency relation probabilities.

One way of estimating parameters of phrase alignment probabilities is using the following equations:

$$
\begin{aligned}
p(F_j|E_i) &= \frac{C(F_j, E_i)}{\sum_k C(F_k, E_i)} \\
p(E_i|F_j) &= \frac{C(F_j, E_i)}{\sum_k C(E_k, F_j)}
\end{aligned} \tag{14}
$$

where $C(F_j, E_i)$ is a frequency of F_j and E_i is aligned.

However, if we use this in our model, the phrase translation probability of the new possible phrase can become extremely high (often it becomes 1). To avoid this problem, we use the equations below for the estimation of phrase translation probability in place of Equation 14:

$$
p(F_j|E_i) = \frac{C(F_j, E_i)}{C(E_i)}, p(E_i|F_j) = \frac{C(F_j, E_i)}{C(F_j)} \tag{15}
$$

$C(E_i)$ is the frequency of the phrase E_i in the training corpus which can be pre-counted. This definition can resolve the problem where the phrase translation probability of the new possible phrase becomes too high.

As for the NULL, we use Equation 14 because we cannot pre-count the frequency of NULL.

Using the estimated phrase alignment probabilities and dependency relation probabilities, we go back to the initial alignment described in Section 3.2.1 iteratively.

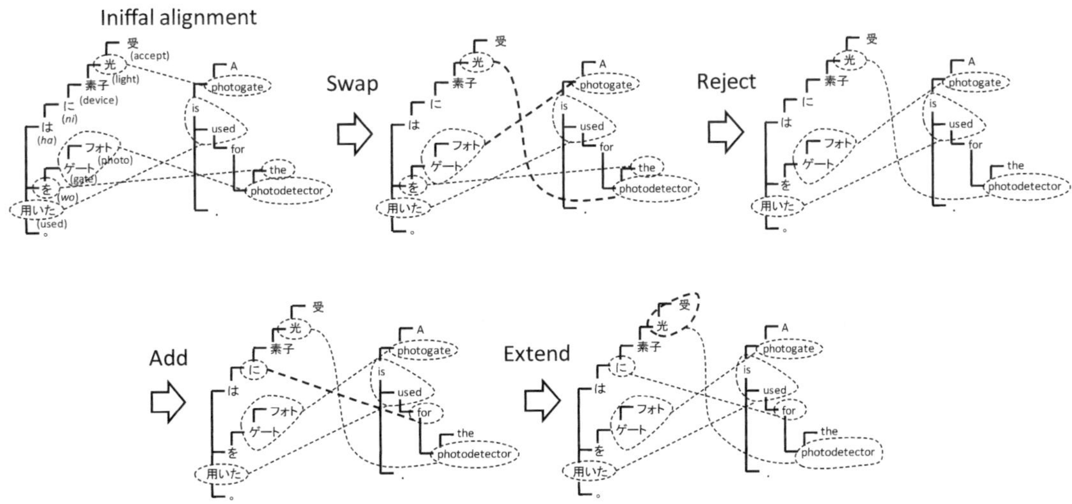

Figure 2: An example of hill-climbing.

4 Experimental Results

We conducted alignment experiments. A JST[1] Japanese-English paper abstract corpus consisting of 1M parallel sentences was used for the model training. This corpus was constructed from a 2M Japanese-English paper abstract corpus by NICT[2] using the method of Uchiyama and Isahara (2007). As gold-standard data, we used 475 sentence pairs which were annotated by hand. The annotations were only sure (S) alignments (there were no possible (P) alignments) (Och and Ney, 2003). The unit of evaluation was word-base for both Japanese and English. We used precision, recall, and F-measure as evaluation criteria.

We conducted two experiments to reveal 1) the contribution of our proposed model compared to the existing models, and 2) the effectiveness of using dependency tree structure and phrases, which are larger alignment units than words. Trainings were run on the original forms of words for both the proposed model and the models used for comparison.

4.1 Comparison with Word Sequential Model

For comparison, we used GIZA++ (Och and Ney, 2003) which implements the prominent sequential word-base statistical alignment model of IBM Models. We conducted word alignment bidirectionally with its default parameters and merged them using three types of symmetrization heuristics (Koehn et al., 2003). The results are shown in Table 2.

[1]http://www.jst.go.jp/

[2]http://www.nict.go.jp/

The result of 'Step 1' uses parameters estimated after 5 iterations of Step 1. The alignment is obtained by the method of initial alignment shown in Section 3.2.1. In 'Step 2-1', the phrase translation probabilities are the same as those in 'Step 1'. In addition, dependency relation probabilities estimated from the 'Step 1' alignment result are used. By comparing 'Step 1' and 'Step 2-1', we can see the effectiveness of dependency relation probability. We performed 5 iterations for Step 2 and calculated the alignment accuracy each time. As a result, the proposed model could achieve a higher F-measure by 1.7 points compared to the sequential model. 'Intersection' achieved best Precision, but its Recall is quite low. 'grow-diag-final-and' achieved best Recall, but its Precision is lower than our best result where the Recall is almost same. Thus, we can say our result is better than sequential word alignment models.

4.2 Effectiveness of Dependency Trees and Phrases

To confirm the effectiveness of dependency trees and phrases, we conducted alignment experiments on the following four conditions:

- Using both dependency trees and phrases (referred to as 'proposed').
- Using dependency trees only.
- Using phrases only.
- Not using dependency trees or phrases (referred to as 'none')

For the conditions which do not use dependency trees, we used positional relations of a sentence as

Table 2: Results of alignment experiment.

	Precision	Recall	F
Step 1	77.55	33.92	47.20
Step 2-1	83.46	40.03	54.11
Step 2-2	87.74	45.37	59.81
Step 2-3	87.62	48.92	62.79
Step 2-4	86.87	50.42	63.81
Step 2-5	85.90	50.75	63.80
Step 2-6	85.54	51.00	**63.90**
Step 2-7	85.18	50.87	63.70
Step 2-8	84.66	50.75	63.46
intersection	**90.34**	34.28	49.71
grow-final-and	81.32	48.85	61.04
grow-diag-final-and	79.39	**51.15**	62.22

Table 3: Effectiveness of dependency trees and phrases (results after 5 iterations in Step 2.)

	Precision	Recall	F
proposed	85.54	**51.00**	**63.90**
dependency tree only	**89.77**	39.47	54.83
phrase only	84.41	47.33	60.65
none	85.07	38.06	52.59

a sequence of words instead of dependency tree relations. The results are shown in Table 3. All the results are the alignment accuracy after 5 iterations of Step 2.

5 Discussion

Table 2 shows that our proposed model could achieve reasonably high accuracy of alignment, and is better than sequential word-base models. As an example, alignment results of a word sequential model are shown in Figure 3. The gray colored cells are the gold-standard alignments, and the black boxes are the outputs of the sequential model. The model failed to resolve the correspondence ambiguities between "非 (*not*) 去勢 (*castrated*) マウス (*mice*)", and "去勢 マウス"; and "non-castrated mice", and "castrated mice" respectively. This is because these words are placed close to each other and are also close to the correspondence "同様に ↔ as" which can be a clue to the word order. Using the tree structure in Figure 4, these words were correctly aligned. This is because in the English tree, the phrase "castrated mice" does not depend on "as", and "non-castrated mice" does. Similarly in the Japanese tree, "非 去勢 マウス" depends on "同様に" and "去勢 マウス" does not.

As mentioned in Section 1, sequential statistical methods, which regard a sentence as a sequence of words, work well for language pairs that are not too different in their language structure. Japanese and English have significantly different structures. One of the issues is that Japanese sentences have a SOV word order, but in English, the word order is SVO, so the dependency relations are often turned over. For language pairs such as Japanese and English, deeper sentence analysis using NLP resources is necessary and useful. Our method is therefore suitable for such language pairs.

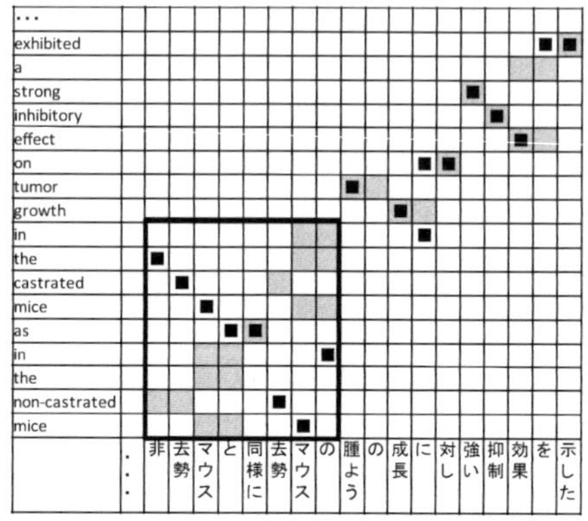

Figure 3: An alignment example of the word sequential model (grow-diag-final-and).

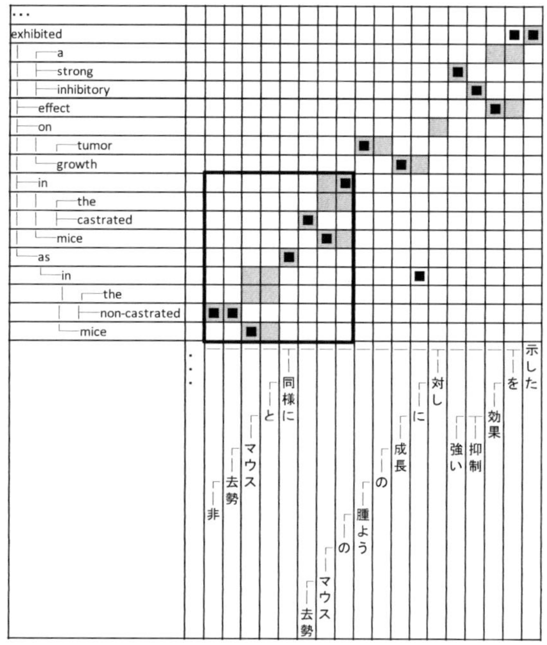

Figure 4: An alignment example of the proposed model.

As another example of an alignment failure by the sequential model, Figure 5 shows the phrase correspondence "受 光 素子 ↔ photodetector", which was correctly found as shown in Figure 6. The pro-

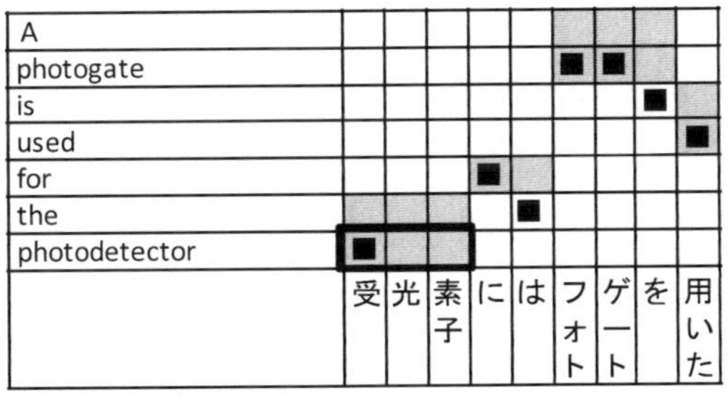

Figure 5: An unsuccessful example of phrase detection in the sequential model (grow-diag-final-and).

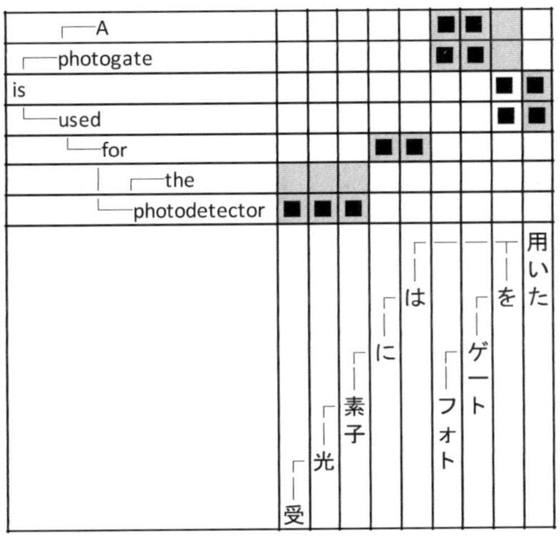

Figure 6: An example of phrase detection in the proposed model.

posed method of generating possible phrases during iterations works well and improves alignment.

From the result of our second experiment, we can see the following points:

1. Phrasal alignment improves the recall, but lowers the precision.
2. By using dependency trees, precision can be improved.
3. We can find a balance point by using both phrasal alignment and dependency trees.

The causes of alignment errors in our model can be summarized into categories. The biggest one is parsing errors. Since our model is highly dependent on the parsing result, the alignments would easily turn out wrong if the parsing result was incorrect.

Sometimes the hill-climbing algorithm could not revise the initial alignment. Most of these cases would happen when one word occurred several times on one side, but some of those occurrences were omitted on the other side. Let's suppose there are two identical words on the source side, but the target side has only one corresponding word. Initial alignment is created without considering the dependencies at all, so it cannot judge which source word should be aligned to the corresponding target word. In this case, the best alignment searching sometimes gets the local solution. This problem could be resolved by considering local dependencies for ambiguous words.

One difficulty is how to handle function words. Function words often do not have exactly corresponding words in the opposite language. Japanese case markers such as "は *(ha)*", "が *(ga)*" (subjective case), "を *(wo)*" (objective case) and so on, and English articles are typical examples of words, that do not have corresponding parts. There is a difference between alignment criteria for function words of gold-standard and our outputs, and it is somewhat difficult to improve alignment accuracy.

6 Conclusion

In this paper, we have proposed a linguistically-motivated probabilistic phrase alignment model based on dependency tree structures. The model incorporates the tree-based reordering model. Experimental results show that the word sequential model does not work well for linguistically different language pairs, and this can be resolved by using syntactic information. We have conducted the experiments only on Japanese-English corpora. To firmly support our claim that syntactic information is important, it is necessary to do more investigation on other language pairs.

Most frequent alignment errors are derived from parsing errors. Because our method depends heavily on structural information, parsing errors easily make the alignment accuracy worse. Although the parsing accuracy is high in general for both Japanese and English, it sometimes outputs incorrect dependency structures because technical or unknown words often appears in scientific papers. This problem could be resolved by introducing parsing probabilities into our model using parsing tools which can output n-best parsing with their parsing probabilities. This will not only improve the alignment accuracy, it will allow revision of the parsing result. Moreover, we need to investigate the contribution of our alignment result to the translation quality.

References

Peter F. Brown, Stephen A. Della Pietra, Vincent J. Della Pietra, and Robert L. Mercer. 1993. The mathematics of statistical machine translation: Parameter estimation. *Association for Computational Linguistics*, 19(2):263–312.

Colin Cherry and Dekang Lin. 2003. A probability model to improve word alignment. In *Proceedings of the 41st Annual Meeting of the Association of Computational Linguistics*, pages 88–95.

Brooke Cowan, Ivona Kučerová, and Michael Collins. 2006. A discriminative model for tree-to-tree translation. In *Proceedings of the 2006 Conference on EMNLP*, pages 232–241, Sydney, Australia, July. Association for Computational Linguistics.

Daniel Gildea. 2003. Loosely tree-based alignment for machine translation. In *Proceedings of the 41st Annual Meeting on ACL*, pages 80–87.

Daisuke Kawahara and Sadao Kurohashi. 2006. A fully-lexicalized probabilistic model for japanese syntactic and case structure analysis. In *Proceedings of the Human Language Technology Conference of the NAACL, Main Conference*, pages 176–183, New York City, USA, June. Association for Computational Linguistics.

Philipp Koehn, Franz J. Och, and Daniel Marcu. 2003. Statistical phrase-based translation. In *HLT-NAACL 2003: Main Proceedings*, pages 127–133.

Sadao Kurohashi, Toshihisa Nakamura, Yuji Matsumoto, and Makoto Nagao. 1994. Improvements of Japanese morphological analyzer JUMAN. In *Proceedings of The International Workshop on Sharable Natural Language*, pages 22–28.

Percy Liang, Ben Taskar, and Dan Klein. 2006. Alignment by agreement. In *Proceedings of the Human Language Technology Conference of the NAACL, Main Conference*, pages 104–111, New York City, USA, June. Association for Computational Linguistics.

Ryan McDonald, Fernando Pereira, Kiril Ribarov, and Jan Hajic. 2005. Non-projective dependency parsing using spanning tree algorithms. In *Proceedings of Human Language Technology Conference and Conference on Empirical Methods in Natural Language Processing*, pages 523–530, Vancouver, British Columbia, Canada, October. Association for Computational Linguistics.

Arul Menezes and Stephen D. Richardson. 2001. A best-first alignment algorithm for automatic extraction of transfer mappings from bilingual corpora. In *Proceedings of the 39th Annual Meeting of the Association for Computational Linguistics (ACL) Workshop on Data-Driven Machine Translation*, pages 39–46.

Toshiaki Nakazawa and Sadao Kurohashi. 2008. Linguistically-motivated tree-based probabilistic phrase alignment. In *In Proceedings of the Eighth Conference of the Association for Machine Translation in the Americas (AMTA2008)*.

Franz Josef Och and Hermann Ney. 2003. A systematic comparison of various statistical alignment models. *Association for Computational Linguistics*, 29(1):19–51.

Chris Quirk, Arul Menezes, and Colin Cherry. 2005. Dependency treelet translation: Syntactically informed phrasal SMT. In *Proceedings of the 43rd Annual Meeting of the Association for Computational Linguistics (ACL'05)*, pages 271–279.

Masao Utiyama and Hitoshi Isahara. 2007. A japanese-english patent parallel corpus. In *MT summit XI*, pages 475–482.

Hideo Watanabe, Sadao Kurohashi, and Eiji Aramaki. 2000. Finding structural correspondences from bilingual parsed corpus for corpus-based translation. In *Proceedings of the 18th International Conference on Computational Linguistics*, pages 906–912.

Kenji Yamada and Kevin Knight. 2001. A syntax-based statistical translation model. In *Proceedings of 39th Annual Meeting of the ACL*, pages 523–530.

Empirical lower bounds on alignment error rates in syntax-based machine translation

Anders Søgaard*
Center for Language Technology
University of Copenhagen
soegaard@hum.ku.dk

Jonas Kuhn†
Dpt. of Linguistics
University of Potsdam
kuhn@ling.uni-potsdam.de

Abstract

The empirical adequacy of synchronous context-free grammars of rank two (2-SCFGs) (Satta and Peserico, 2005), used in syntax-based machine translation systems such as Wu (1997), Zhang et al. (2006) and Chiang (2007), in terms of what alignments they induce, has been discussed in Wu (1997) and Wellington et al. (2006), but with a one-sided focus on so-called "inside-out alignments". Other alignment configurations that cannot be induced by 2-SCFGs are identified in this paper, and their frequencies across a wide collection of hand-aligned parallel corpora are examined. Empirical lower bounds on two measures of alignment error rate, i.e. the one introduced in Och and Ney (2000) and one where only complete translation units are considered, are derived for 2-SCFGs and related formalisms.

1 Introduction

Syntax-based approaches to machine translation typically use synchronous grammars to recognize or produce translation equivalents. The synchronous production rules are typically learned from alignment structures (Wu, 1997; Zhang and Gildea, 2004; Chiang, 2007) or from alignment structures and derivation trees for the source string (Yamada and Knight, 2001; Zhang and Gildea, 2004). They are also used for inducing alignments (Wu, 1997; Zhang and Gildea, 2004).

It is for all three reasons, i.e. translation, induction from alignment structures and induction of alignment structures, important that the synchronous grammars are expressive enough to induce all the alignment structures found in hand-aligned gold standard parallel corpora (Wellington et al., 2006). Such alignments are supposed to reflect the structure of translations, typically contain fewer errors and are used to evaluate automatically induced alignments.

In this paper it is shown that the synchronous grammars used in Wu (1997), Zhang et al. (2006) and Chiang (2007) are not expressive enough to do that. The synchronous grammars used in these systems are, formally, synchronous context-free grammars of rank two (2-SCFGs), or equivalently (normal form) inversion transduction grammars (ITGs).[1] The notion of *rank* is defined as the maximum number of constituents aligned by a production rule, i.e. the maximum number of distinct indeces. Our results will be extended to slight extensions of 2-SCFGs, incl. the extension of ITGs proposed by Zens and Ney (2003) (xITGs), synchronous tree substitution grammars of rank two (2-STSGs) (Eisner, 2003; Shieber, 2007), i.e. where tree pairs include at most two linked pairs of nonterminals, and synchronous tree-adjoining grammars of rank two

*This work was done while the first author was a Senior Researcher at the Dpt. of Linguistics, University of Potsdam, supported by the German Research Foundation in the Emmy Noether project *Ptolemaios* on grammar learning from parallel corpora; and while he was a Postdoctoral Researcher at the ISV Computational Linguistics Group, Copenhagen Business School, supported by the Danish Research Foundation in the project *Efficient syntax- and semantics-based machine translation*.

†The second author is supported by the German Research Foundation in the Emmy Noether project *Ptolemaios* on grammar learning from parallel corpora.

[1] 2-SCFGs allow distinct LHS nonterminals, while ITGs do not; but for any 2-SCFG an equivalent ITG can be constructed by creating a cross-product of nonterminals from two sides.

Proceedings of SSST-3, Third Workshop on Syntax and Structure in Statistical Translation, pages 19–27,
Boulder, Colorado, June 2009.

(2-STAGs) (Shieber and Schabes, 1990; Harbusch and Poller, 1996; Nesson et al., 2008). The overall frequency of alignment structures that cannot be induced by these approaches is examined across a wide collection of hand-aligned parallel corpora. Empirical lower bounds on the coverage of the systems are derived from our results.

Our notion of an alignment structure is standard. Words can be aligned to multiple words. Unaligned nodes are permitted. Maximally connected subgraphs are called translation units. There is one more choice to make in the context of many-to-many alignments, namely whether the alignment relation is such that if $w_i|w'_k$ and $w_i|w'_l$, resp., are aligned, and $w_j|w'_k$ are aligned too, then $w_j|w'_l$ are also aligned. If so, the alignment structure is divided into complete translation units. Such alignment structures are therefore called *complete*; in Goutte et al. (2004), alignment structures with this property are said to be closed under transitivity. An alignment structure is simply written as a sequence of alignments, e.g. $\langle w_i|w'_k, w_i|w'_l, w_j|w'_k, w_j|w'_k\rangle$, or, alternatively, as sequences of (possibly discontinuous) translation units, e.g. $\langle w_i w_j|w'_k w'_l\rangle$.

A translation unit induced by a synchronous grammar is a set of terminals that are recognized or generated simultaneously. Consequently, synchronous grammars can only induce complete alignment structures (by transitivity of simultaneity).[2]

Syntax-based approaches to machine translations are commonly evaluated in terms of their alignment error rate (AER) on one or more parallel corpora (Och and Ney, 2000; Zhang and Gildea, 2004). The AER, in the case where all alignments are sure alignments, is

$$\text{AER} = 1 - \frac{2|S_A \cap G_A|}{|S_A| + |G_A|}$$

where G_A are the gold standard alignments, and S_A the alignments produced by the system.

AER has been criticized by Fraser and Marcu (2007). They show that AER does not penalize unequal precision and recall when a distinction between sure and possible alignments is made. Since no such distinction is assumed below, the classical definition is used.

We introduce also the notion of *translation unit error rate* (TUER), which is defined as

$$\text{TUER} = 1 - \frac{2|S_U \cap G_U|}{|S_U| + |G_U|}$$

where G_U are the translation units in the gold standard, and S_U the translation units produced by the system. In other words, what is measured is a system's ability to predict translation units relative to the Gold standard, not just its ability to predict alignments. If the system only gets part of a translation unit right, it is not rewarded.

In the context of many-to-many alignments, this measure may tell us more about translation quality than AER. Consider, for instance, the small children's book discourse in Danish:

(1) *Mads og Mette lægger tal*
Mads CONJ Mette put.FIN.PRES number.PL
sammen.
together
'Mads and Mette add numbers.'

(2) *Mads og Mette lægger tal*
Mads CONJ Mette put.FIN.PRES number.PL
sammen hver dag.
together every day
'Mads and Mette add numbers every day.'

(3) *Mads og Mette kan godt*
Mads CONJ Mette can.FIN.PRES good
lide at addere.
like.INF to add.INF
'Mads and Mette like to add.'

(4) *Mette spørger ofte:*
Mette ask.FIN.PRES often:
Skal vi addere
Shall.FIN.FUT/PRES PRON.PL.1 add.INF
sammen?
together
'Mette often asks: Do you want to add together?'

Say (1-4) and the English translations are a parallel corpus on which we would like to evaluate an aligner or a statistical machine translation system. Say also that the test corpus has been aligned. Let the first three sentences be our training data and (4) our test data.

[2] One of the hand-aligned parallel corpora used in our experiments, the one also used in Padó and Lapata (2006), includes incomplete alignment structures.

Note that the words *lægger ... sammen* form a discontinuous translation unit ('add'). Say our aligner aligned only *sammen* and *add*, but not *lægger* and *add*. This would mean that the alignments or translations of *add* would most likely be associated with the following probabilities:

.66 (*add, sammen*)
.33 (*add, addere*)

which again means that our system is likely to arrive at the wrong alignment or translation in (4). Nevertheless these alignments are rewarded in AER. TUER, on the other hand, reflects the intuition that unless you get the entire translation unit it's better to get nothing at all.

The hand-aligned parallel corpora in our experiments come from the Copenhagen Dependency Treebank (Buch-Kromann, 2007), for five different language pairs, the German-English parallel corpus used in Padó and Lapata (2006), and the six parallel corpora of the first 100 sentences of Europarl (Koehn, 2005) for different language pairs documented in Graca et al. (2008). Consequently, our experiments include a total of 12 parallel corpora. The biggest parallel corpus consists of 4,729 sentence pairs; the smallest of 61 sentence pairs. The average size is 541 sentence pairs. The six parallel corpora documented in Graca et al. (2008) use sure and possible alignments; in our experiments, as already mentioned, the two types of alignments are treated alike.[3]

Sect. 2 discusses the frequency of inside-out alignments in our hand-aligned corpora, whereas Sect. 3 is about complex translation units. Sect. 4 briefly introduces formalisms for syntax-based machine translation, but some prior knowledge is assumed. Sect. 5 brings the three sections together and presents lower bounds on the coverage of the systems discussed in Sect. 4, obtained by inspection of the results in Sect. 2 and 3. Sect. 6 compares our results to related work, in particular Zens and Ney (2003).

2 Inside-out alignments

Wu (1997) identified so-called inside-out alignments, two alignment configurations that cannot be induced by binary synchronous context-free grammars; these alignment configurations, while infrequent in language pairs such as English–French (Cherry and Lin, 2006; Wellington et al., 2006), have been argued to be frequent in other language pairs, incl. English–Chinese (Wellington et al., 2006) and English–Spanish (Lepage and Denoual, 2005). While our main focus is on configurations that involve discontinuous translation units, the frequencies of inside-out alignments in our parallel corpora are also reported. Recall that inside-out alignments are of the form (or upside-down):

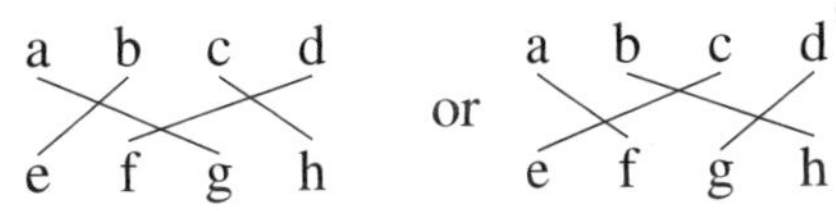

Our findings are summarized in Figure 1. Note that there is some variation across the corpora. The fact that there are no inside-out alignments in corpora 2–4 may be because annotators of these corpora have been very conservative, i.e. there are many unaligned nodes; the first corpus, which is also part of the Danish Dependency Treebank, also has very few inside-out alignments. It is not entirely clear to us if this has to do with the languages in question or the annotation guide lines (cf. Danish–Spanish).

In the Danish–Spanish corpus and in the English–German corpus the number of inside-out alignments is very high. This, to some extent, has to do with the number of words that are aligned to multiple words.

[3]The annotations of the parallel corpora differ in format and consistency. In fact the empirical lower bounds obtained below are lower bounds in two senses: (i) they are lower bounds on TUERs because TUERs may be significantly higher than the empirical lower bounds found here, and (ii) they are lower bounds in the sense that there may be hidden instances of the configurations in question in the parallel corpora. Most seriously, our search algorithms only sort alignments, but not their elements; instead they assume that their elements are listed in chronological order. Sometimes, but rarely, this is not the case. Consider, for instance, file 1497, line 12 in the Danish–Spanish parallel corpus in the Copenhagen Dependency Treebank:

<align out=”a56” type=”” in=”b30+b32+b8” outsign=”af” insign=”del de de”/>

This is a translation unit. The word in position 56 in the source string is aligned to the words in positions 8, 30 and 32 in the target string, but note that the target string words do not appear in chronological order. In some cases our algorithms take care of this; they do not, however, in general search all possible combinations of words and alignments, but rely on the linear order of the annotation. This was necessary to do relatively efficient queries. The effect, however, is that our results are lower than the actual frequencies in the parallel corpora. They are in this sense also lower bounds.

	Snt.	TUs	IO	IO-m	IO-m/Snt.
Danish–English:	4,729	110,511	28	4	0.001
Danish–German:	61	1,026	0	0	0
Danish–Italian:	181	2,182	0	0	0
Danish–Russian:	61	618	0	0	0
Danish–Spanish:	710	6,110	2,562	158	0.223
English–German	987	68,760	191,490	1,178	1.194
English–French:	100	937	2,651	80	0.800
English-Portuguese:	100	941	3,856	66	0.660
English–Spanish:	100	950	2,287	67	0.670
Portuguese–French:	100	915	3,643	84	0.840
Portuguese–Spanish:	100	991	1,194	58	0.580
Spanish–French	100	975	1,390	61	0.610

Figure 1: Frequency of inside-out alignments.

Say, in the case of English–German, each inside-out alignment is made out of eight two-word translation units. There are 1,178 inside-out alignment *modulo* translation units, i.e. when one or more inside-out alignments over the same eight translation units only count as one; this means that there would be $2^8 \times 1,178 : 301,568$ inside-out alignments in total. The actual number $(191,491)$ is smaller, but comparable.

The first example in the English–German corpus, from sentence 2, illustrates this point. The sentences are:

(5) Mr Jonckheer, I would like to thank you just as warmly for your report on the seventh survey on State aid in the European Union .

(6) Ebenso herzlich möchte ich Ihnen, Herr Jonckheer, für Ihren Bericht über den siebenten Bericht über staatliche Beihilfen in der Europäischen Union danken (24).

and the alignment structure is (commas count):

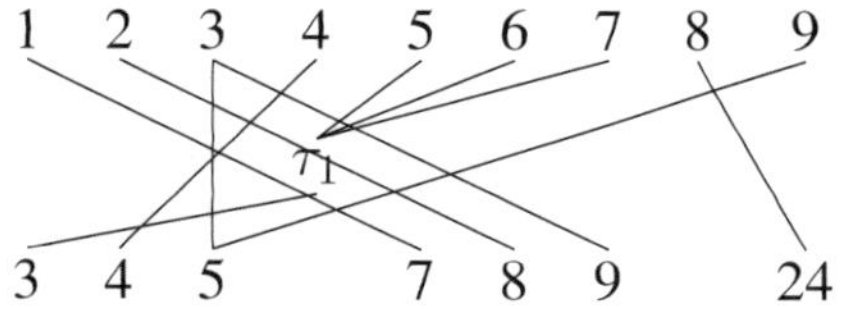

The aligned translation units are:[4]

[4]Note that the alignment 3|5 is probably a mistake made by the annotator. It should, it seems, be 3|6. Note also that this alignment is not involved in any of the inside-out alignments.

⟨Mr|Herr⟩ ⟨Jonckheer|Jonckheer⟩
⟨,|Ihnen ...,⟩ ⟨I|ich⟩
⟨would like to|möchte⟩ ⟨thank|danken⟩
⟨you|Ihnen⟩

Note that the following sets of alignments make up distinct inside-out alignments *modulo* translation units:

$$\{\langle 1|7,4|4,8|24,9|5\rangle, \langle 2|8,4|4,8|24,9|5\rangle, \langle 3|9,4|4,8|24,9|5\rangle, \langle 1|7,5|3,8|24,9|5\rangle, \langle 2|8,5|3,8|24,9|5\rangle, \langle 3|9,5|3,8|24,9|5\rangle\}$$

The following sets of alignments in addition make up distinct inside-out alignments, but the new alignments 6|3 and 7|3 are from the same translation unit as 5|3:

$$\{\langle 1|7,6|3,8|24,9|5\rangle, \langle 2|8,6|3,8|24,9|5\rangle, \langle 3|9,6|3,8|24,9|5\rangle, \langle 1|7,6|3,8|24,9|5\rangle, \langle 2|8,6|3,8|24,9|5\rangle, \langle 3|9,6|3,8|24,9|5\rangle\}$$

Consequently, the alignment of sentences (5) and (6) in the English–German parallel corpus contains 12 inside-out alignments, but only six inside-out alignments *modulo* translation units.

3 Cross-serial discontinuous translation units

A discontinuous translation unit (DTU) is a translation unit where either the substring of source string words or the substring of target string words that occur in it, is discontinuous, i.e. there is a gap in it.

Since translation units are induced by simultaneous recognition, it is necessary for synchronous grammars to have rules that introduce multiple source side terminals and/or multiple target side terminals with at least one intervening nonterminal to induce DTUs. A DTU with multiple gaps in the same side is called a multigap DTU; it is easy to see that binary grammars cannot induce multigap DTUs with more than two gaps.

A sequence of DTUs is said to be *cross-serial* if it is of the following form (or upside-down):

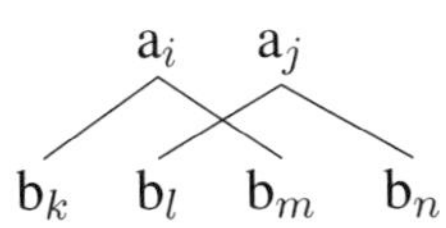

Call any sequence of cross-serial DTUs a cross-serial DTU (CDTU). So a CDTU is an alignment configuration such that the source-side, resp. target-side, contains four tokens b_k, b_l, b_m, b_n such that (i) $b_k \prec b_l \prec b_m \prec b_n$, (ii) b_k and b_m belong to the same translation unit T, and b_l and b_n belong to the same translation unit T', and (iii) T and T' are distinct translation units. The inability of ITGs, xITGs and 2-STSGs to induce CDTUs follows from the observation that if b_k and b_m in the above are generated or recognized simultatenously in any of these formalisms, b_l and b_n cannot be generated or recognized simulaneously. This is a straight-forward consequence of the context-freeness of the component grammars.

The distinction between CDTUs and CDTUs *modulo* translation units (CDTU-ms) is again important. The number of CDTU-ms is the number of CDTUs such that all CDTUs differ by at most one translation unit. The English–German parallel corpus, for example, contains 15,717 CDTUs, but only 2,079 CDTU-ms. Since our evaluation measure is TUER, we only systematically counted the occurrences of CDTU-ms. In a few cases, the number of CDTUs was extracted too. In general, it was about eight times higher than the number of CDTU-ms.

Our findings are summarized in Figure 2. There is again variation, but the average ratio of CDTU-ms is 0.514, i.e. there is a CDTU-m in about every second aligned sentence pair.

4 Syntax-based machine translation

Syntax-directed translation schemas (SDTSs) were originally introduced by Culik (1966) and studied formally by Aho and Ullman (1972), who stressed the importance of using only binary SDTSs for efficiency reasons,[5] and later led to the development of a number of near-equivalent theories, incl. 2-SCFGs and (normal form) ITGs. Henceforth, we will refer to this class of near-equivalent theories as ITGs (see footnote 1). This also means that production rules have at most one source-side and one target-side terminal on the RHS (see below).

It is the ability of ITGs to induce alignments that is our main focus. Related work includes Wu (1997), Zens and Ney (2003) and Wellington et al. (2006). Our results will also be extended to xITGs, 2-STSGs and 2-STAGs. $\mathcal{O}(|G|n^6)$ time recognition algorithms are known for ITGs, xITGs and 2-STSGs. 2-STAGs ($\mathcal{O}(|G|n^{12})$) are more complex.

The production rules in ITGs are of the following form (Wu, 1997), with a notation similar to what is typically used for SDTSs and SCFGs in the right column:

$$
\begin{array}{l|l}
A \rightarrow [BC] & A \rightarrow \langle B^1C^2, B^1C^2 \rangle \\
A \rightarrow \langle BC \rangle & A \rightarrow \langle B^1C^2, C^2B^1 \rangle \\
A \rightarrow e \mid f & A \rightarrow \langle e, f \rangle \\
A \rightarrow e \mid \epsilon & A \rightarrow \langle e, \epsilon \rangle \\
A \rightarrow \epsilon \mid f & A \rightarrow \langle \epsilon, f \rangle
\end{array}
$$

It is important to note that RHSs of production rules have at most one source-side and one target-side terminal symbol. This prevents induction of multiword translation units in any straight-forward way. xITGs (Zens and Ney, 2003) in part solves this problem. All production rules in ITGs can be production rules in xITGs, but xITG production rules can also be of the following form:

$$A \quad \rightarrow \quad [e/f_1 A \epsilon/f_2] \mid \langle e/f_1 A \epsilon/f_2 \rangle$$

Note, however, that these production rules still do not enable double-sided DTUs, i.e. DTUs that translate into DTUs. Such, however, occur relatively frequently in hand-aligned parallel corpora, e.g. 148 times in the Danish–Spanish corpus.

There is no room for detailed introductions of the more complex formalisms, but briefly their differences can be summarized as follows:

The move from ITGs to 2-STSGs is relatively simple. All production rules in ITGs characterize

[5]The hierarchy of SDTSs of rank k is non-collapsing, and the recognition problem without a fixed rank is NP-hard (Aho and Ullman, 1972; Rambow and Satta, 1994). See Zhang et al. (2006) for an efficient binarization algorithm.

	Snt.	TUs	DTUs	DTUs/Snt.	CDTU-ms	CDTU-ms/Snt.
Danish–English:	4,729	110,511	1,801	0.381	6	0.001
Danish–German:	61	1,026	43	0.705	0	0
Danish–Italian:	181	2,182	63	0.348	1	0.006
Danish–Russian:	61	618	27	0.443	0	0
Danish–Spanish:	710	6,693	779	1.097	121	0.170
English–German	650	68,760	5,062	7.788	2,079	3.199
English–French:	100	937	95	0.950	38	0.380
English-Portuguese:	100	941	100	1.000	85	0.850
English–Spanish:	100	950	90	0.900	50	0.500
Portuguese–French:	100	915	77	0.770	27	0.270
Portuguese–Spanish:	100	991	80	0.800	55	0.550
Spanish–French	100	975	74	0.740	24	0.240

Figure 2: Frequency of cross-serial DTUs.

binary trees of depth 1. It is said that this is the domain of locality in ITGs. 2-STSGs extend the domain of locality to arbitrarily big trees. 2-STSGs are collections of ordered pairs of aligned trees with at most two pairs of linked nonterminals. The leaf nodes in the trees may be decorated by terminals or insertion slots where subtrees can be "plugged in". This is exactly what is meant by tree substitution. It is assumed that all terminals in a tree pair constitute a translation unit. There exists a $\mathcal{O}(|G|n^6)$ time parsing algorithm for 2-STSGs. 2-STSGs induce DTUs, double-sided DTUs and DTUs with at most two gaps, but *not* inside-out alignments, CDTUs and multigap DTUs with more than two gaps.

The substitution operation on elementary trees is supplied with an adjunction operation in 2-STAGs (Shieber and Schabes, 1990; Harbusch and Poller, 1996; Nesson et al., 2008). In adjunction, auxiliary trees, i.e. elementary trees with a designated leaf node labeled by a nonterminal identical to the nonterminal that labels the root node, extend the derived tree by expanding one of its nodes. If an auxiliary tree t, with a root node and a leaf node both labeled A, is adjoined at some node n also labeled A in a derived tree t', the subtree s' (of t') rooted at n is replaced by t, and s' is then inserted at the leaf node of t. In 2-STAGs, paired nodes across the source-side and target-side trees are simultaneously expanded by either substitution or adjunction. A $\mathcal{O}(|G|n^{12})$ parsing algorithm can be deviced for 2-STAGs using the techniques in Seki et al. (1991). The following 2-STAG translates Swiss-style cross-serial dependencies $\{wa^mb^nxc^md^ny\}$ into $\{w(ac)^mx(bd)^ny\}$ and thus induces cross-serial DTUs whenever $m,n \geq 1$ (superscripts are pairings).

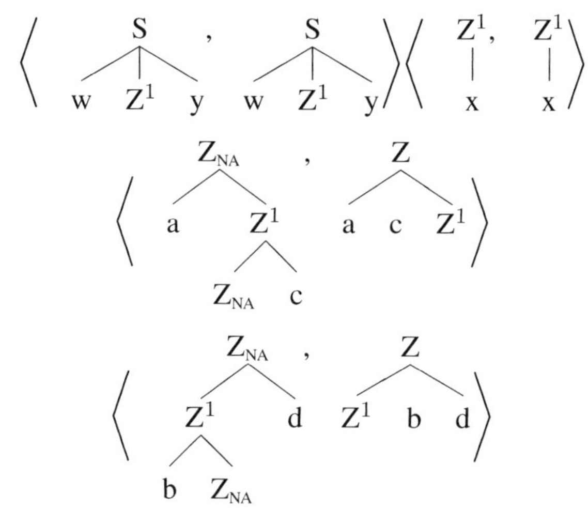

2-STAGs thus induce DTUs, double-sided DTUs, CDTUs, but not multigap DTUs with more than two gaps. 2-STAGs also induce inside-out alignments. Consider, for instance:

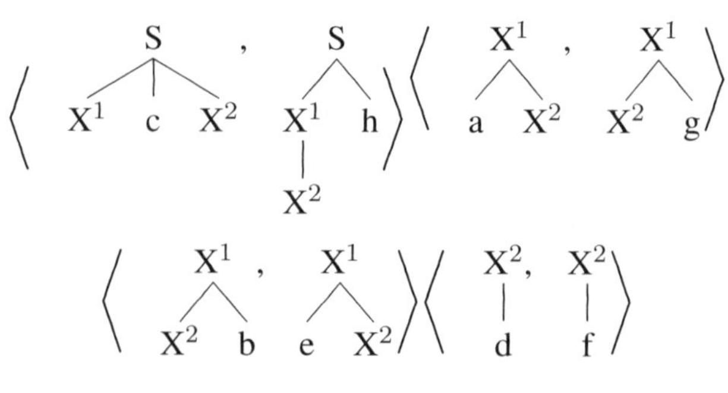

It is left for the reader to verify that this grammar induces the first of the two inside-out alignment configurations in Sect. 2.

5 Lower bounds on translation unit error rates

The ratio of inside-out alignments over TUs is a lower bound on the TUER for the binary versions of all the formalisms listed above, except 2-STAGs.

	IOs/TUs
Danish–English	0
Danish–German	0
Danish–Italian	0
Danish–Russian	0
Danish–Spanish	0.026
English–German	0.017
English–French	0.085
English–Portuguese	0.070
English–Spanish	0.070
Portuguese–French	0.092
Portuguese–Spanish	0.059
Spanish–French	0.063

For ITGs the ratio of DTUs over TUs is a lower bound on the TUER.

	DTUs/TUs
Danish–English	0.016
Danish–German	0.042
Danish–Italian	0.029
Danish–Russian	0.044
Danish–Spanish	0.121
English–German	0.074
English–French	0.101
English–Portuguese	0.106
English–Spanish	0.095
Portuguese–French	0.084
Portuguese–Spanish	0.081
Spanish–French	0.076

This is a considerable lower bound in itself, even for closely related languages such as Danish–German (4.2%) or Portuguese–Spanish (8.1%), which seems to have motivated research on extensions of ITGs (Zens and Ney, 2003). The ratio of CDTU-ms over TUs is a lower bound on the TUER for all the formalisms listed, except 2-STAGs:

	CDTU-ms/TUs
Danish–English	0
Danish–German	0
Danish–Italian	0.001
Danish–Russian	0
Danish–Spanish	0.018
English–German	0.030
English–French	0.041
English–Portuguese	0.090
English–Spanish	0.053
Portuguese–French	0.030
Portuguese–Spanish	0.056
Spanish–French	0.025

From these tables, empirical lower bounds on TUERs can be derived. ITGs, for instance, will have a TUER of at least $2.6\% + 12.1\% = 14.7\%$ for Danish–Spanish,[6] while 2-STSGs, ignoring problems caused by multigap DTUs with more than two gaps, will have a TUER of at least $7.0\% + 9.0\% = 16.0\%$ for English–Portuguese. Similarly lower bounds on AER for ITGs can be obtained by summing IOs/As, i.e. the number of inside-out alignments over the number of alignments, DTUs/As and CDTUs/As; for 2-STSGs, the lower bounds are given by IOs/As + CDTUs/As; and so on. Even 2-STAGs exclude alignments found in the data, namely multigap DTUs. The number of multigap DTUs (MDTUs) in the corpora documented in Graca et al. (2008) range from 3–11 (in a 100 sentences) with an average of 5.8. Exact results for each formalism that include double-sided DTUs and multigap DTUs will be included in a future publication, but it is clear to us that both configurations are less frequent than inside-out alignments and CDTUs. In the Danish–Spanish parallel corpus the number of DTUs with three or more gaps is 448 out of which 182 are CDTUs. In the English–German parallel corpus, the numbers are, resp., 2,529 and 996.

[6] It was recently suggested to us by a colleague that the lower bounds need not be additive. It is, theoretically, possible that the errors associated with CDTUs subsume some of the errors associated with inside-out alignments, i.e. that it is possible to remove one alignment or translation unit from the Gold standard alignment structure such that both the CDTU-ms count goes down by one, and the inside-out alignment count goes down by one. It is left for future work to estimate this bias, but it seems to us that such subsumptions will be infrequent.

6 Related work

Zens and Ney (2003) used GIZA++ to word-align the Verbmobil task (English and German) and the Canadian Hansards task (English and French) and tested the coverage of ITGs and xITGs, i.e. the ratio of the number of alignment configurations that could be induced by the theories and the sentences in the two tasks. The results are presented below:

	ITG	xITG
Verbmobil (G→E)	91.6%	96.5%
Verbmobil (E→G)	87.0%	96.9%
Can. Hansards (F→E)	81.3%	96.1%
Can. Hansards (E→F)	73.6%	95.6%

Note that the average differences in coverage between ITGs and xITGs for English-German (7.4%) and English–French (18.4%) are comparable to the DTUs/TUs ratios for English–German (7.4%), resp. English–French (10.1%) in our parallel corpora. Compare also the average error rate of xITGs for English and German (3.3%) and English and French (4.15%) to the CDTU-ms/TUs ratios for English–German (3.0%) and English–French (4.1%).

This data provides strong support that inside-out alignments and cross-serial DTUs are the main theoretical challenge for syntax-based machine translation; in addition, training is a major challenge (Zhang and Gildea, 2004). In real-life applications, AERs and TUERs will be significantly higher than the empirical lower bounds obtained here, e.g. 40% for Chinese–English in Zhang and Gildea (2004), but in principal future results should converge on them.

7 Discussion

In machine translation, as in all other branches of computer science, there is a trade-off between expressivity and complexity. The results presented here, namely that classes of alignment structures excluded by syntax-based translation systems, occur frequently in hand-aligned parallel corpora, could be taken to indicate that more expressive formalisms are needed. This at least seems to be the case to the extent alignment error rates are reasonable measures of the adequacy of syntax-based machine translation systems. On the other hand parsing complexities in syntax-based machine translation are very high already, i.e. $\mathcal{O}(|G|n^6)$ and higher. Consequently, it is not advisable to gain more expressivity at the expense of parsing complexity. This need not be necessary either, however. There are at least two other possibilities:

- Either the cake can be cut differently, i.e. to exclude other classes of alignment structures that occur less frequently. This idea has to the best of our knowledge not been explored in the context of syntax-based machine translation.
- It is also possible to design formalisms for syntax-based machine translation that induce all possible alignment structures and maintain a reasonable parsing complexity ($\mathcal{O}(|G|n^6)$), e.g. Søgaard (2008b); but as noted by Søgaard (2008a) the gain in expressivity is at the expense of the complexity of learning. Finally, it can be shown that there are no computable tight estimators for the probabilistic extension of the formalism introduced in Søgaard (2008b).[7]

8 Conclusion

It was shown how the frequency of certain classes of alignment structures induce empirical lower bounds on the alignment error rates that can be obtained with these systems. Some of these lower bounds are quite significant, e.g. 14.7% (TUER) for ITGs wrt. Danish–Spanish and 17.6% wrt. Portuguese-French. Slightly lower, but still significant, bounds exist for more complex formalisms such as 2-STSGs and 2-STAGs.

[7] Two other challenges for this type of approach are: (i) The use of intersection in Søgaard (2008b) to induce inside-out alignments and cross-serial DTUs seems to miss important generalizations; see Chiang (2004) for a similar point in the context of parsing. (ii) If the class of alignment structures is restricted in any natural way, i.e. to $1:1$ alignments, the problem whether there exists a possible alignment given two sentences and a grammar becomes NP-hard (Søgaard, 2009). NB: The undecidability of computing tight estimators was pointed out to us by Mark-Jan Nederhof (p.c.), but Alexander Clark (p.c.) and others have suggested that pseudo-tight estimators can be used in practice.

References

Alfred Aho and Jeffrey Ullman. 1972. *The theory of parsing, translation and compiling*. Prentice-Hall, London, England.

Matthias Buch-Kromann. 2007. Computing translation units and quantifying parallelism in parallel dependency treebanks. In *ACL'07, Linguistic Annotation Workshop*, pages 69–76.

Colin Cherry and Dekang Lin. 2006. A comparison of syntactically motivated word alignment spaces. In *EACL'06*, pages 145–152, Trento, Italy.

David Chiang. 2004. Uses and abuses of intersected languages. In *TAG+'04*, Vancouver, Canada.

David Chiang. 2007. Hierarchical phrase-based translation. *Computational Linguistics*, 33(2):201–228.

K. Culik. 1966. Well translatable languages and Algol-like languages. In T. Steel, editor, *Formal languages and description languages*, pages 76–85. N. Holland Press, Amsterdam, the Netherlands.

Jason Eisner. 2003. Learning non-isomorphic tree mappings for machine translation. In *ACL'03*, pages 205–208, Sapporo, Japan.

Alexander Fraser and Daniel Marcu. 2007. Measuring word alignment quality for statistical machine translation. *Computational Linguistics*, 33(3):293–303.

Cyril Goutte, Kenji Yamada, and Eric Gaussier. 2004. Aligning words using matrix factorisation. In *ACL'04*, pages 502–509, Barcelona, Spain.

Joao Graca, Joana Pardal, Luísa Coheur, and Diamantino Caseiro. 2008. Building a golden collection of parallel multi-language word alignments. In *LREC'08*, Marrakech, Morocco.

Karin Harbusch and Peter Poller. 1996. Structural translation with synchronous tree-adjoining grammars in Verbmobil. Technical Report Verbmobil 184, Universität Koblenz-Landau/DFKI GmbH, Koblenz, Germany.

Philipp Koehn. 2005. Europarl: a parallel corpus for statistical machine translation. In *MT-Summit'05*, pages 79–86, Phuket, Thailand.

Yves Lepage and Etienne Denoual. 2005. Purest ever example-based machine translation. *Machine Translation*, 19(3–4):251–282.

Rebecca Nesson, Giorgio Satta, and Stuart Shieber. 2008. Optimal k-arization of synchronous tree-adjoining grammar. In *TAG+'08*, Tübingen, Germany.

Franz Och and Hermann Ney. 2000. A comparison of alignment models for statistical machine translation. In *COLING'00*, pages 1086–1090, Saarbrücken, Germany.

Sebastian Padó and Mirella Lapata. 2006. Optimal constituent alignment with edge covers for semantic projection. In *ACL-COLING'06*, pages 1161–1168.

Owen Rambow and Giorgio Satta. 1994. A two-dimensional hierarchy for parallel rewriting systems. Technical report, University of Philadelphia, Philadelphia, Pennsylvania.

Giorgio Satta and Enoch Peserico. 2005. Some computational complexity results for synchronous context-free grammars. In *HLT-EMNLP'05*, pages 803–810, Vancouver, Canada.

Hiroyuki Seki, Takashi Matsumura, Mamoru Fujii, and Tadao Kasami. 1991. On multiple context-free grammars. *Theoretical Computer Science*, 88(2):191–229.

Stuart Shieber and Yves Schabes. 1990. Synchronous tree-adjoining grammars. In *COLING'90*, pages 253–258, Helsinki, Finland.

Stuart Shieber. 2007. Probabilistic synchronous tree-adjoining grammars for machine translation. In *SSST'07*, pages 88–95, Rochester, New York.

Anders Søgaard. 2008a. Learning context-sensitive synchronous rules. In *EAMT'08*, pages 168–173, Hamburg, Germany.

Anders Søgaard. 2008b. Range concatenation grammars for translation. In *COLING'08*, pages 103–106, Manchester, England.

Anders Søgaard. 2009. The complexity of restricted alignment problems in two formalisms for syntax-based machine translation. In *SSST'09*, Boulder, Colorado. To appear.

Benjamin Wellington, Sonjia Waxmonsky, and Dan Melamed. 2006. Empirical lower bounds on the complexity of translational equivalence. In *ACL'06*, pages 977–984, Sydney, Australia.

Dekai Wu. 1997. Stochastic inversion transduction grammars and bilingual parsing of parallel corpora. *Computational Linguistics*, 23(3):377–403.

Kenji Yamada and Kevin Knight. 2001. A syntax-based statistical translation model. In *ACL'01*, pages 531–538, Toulouse, France.

Richard Zens and Hermann Ney. 2003. A comparative study on reordering constraints in statistical machine translation. In *ACL'03*, pages 144–151, Sapporo, Japan.

Hao Zhang and Daniel Gildea. 2004. Syntax-based alignment: supervised or unsupervised? In *COLING'04*, pages 418–424, Geneva, Switzerland.

Hao Zhang, Liang Huang, Daniel Gildea, and Kevin Knight. 2006. Synchronous binarization for machine translation. In *NAACL-HLT'06*, pages 256–263, New York, New York.

Improving Phrase-Based Translation via Word Alignments from Stochastic Inversion Transduction Grammars

Markus SAERS

Dept. of Linguistics and Philology
Uppsala University
Sweden
markus.saers@lingfil.uu.se

Dekai WU
Human Language Technology Center
Dept. of Computer Science & Engineering
HKUST
Hong Kong
dekai@cs.ust.hk

Abstract

We argue that learning word alignments through a compositionally-structured, joint process yields higher phrase-based translation accuracy than the conventional heuristic of intersecting conditional models. Flawed word alignments can lead to flawed phrase translations that damage translation accuracy. Yet the IBM word alignments usually used today are known to be flawed, in large part because IBM models (1) model reordering by allowing unrestricted movement of words, rather than constrained movement of compositional units, and therefore must (2) attempt to compensate via directed, asymmetric distortion and fertility models. The conventional heuristics for attempting to recover from the resulting alignment errors involve estimating two directed models in opposite directions and then intersecting their alignments – to make up for the fact that, in reality, word alignment is an inherently joint relation. A natural alternative is provided by Inversion Transduction Grammars, which estimate the joint word alignment relation directly, eliminating the need for any of the conventional heuristics. We show that this alignment ultimately produces superior translation accuracy on BLEU, NIST, and METEOR metrics over three distinct language pairs.

1 Introduction

In this paper we argue that word alignments learned through a compositionally-structured, joint process are able to significantly improve the training of phrase-based translation systems, leading to higher translation accuracy than the conventional heuristic of intersecting conditional models. Today, statistical machine translation (SMT) systems perform at state-of-the-art levels; their ability to weigh different translation hypotheses against each other to find an optimal solution has proven to be a great asset. What sets various SMT systems apart are the models employed to determine what to consider optimal. The most common systems today consist of phrase-based models, where chunks of texts are substituted and rearranged to produce the output sentence.

Our premise is that certain flawed word alignments can lead to flawed phrase translations that in turn damage translation accuracy, since word alignment is the basis for learning phrase translations in phrase-based SMT systems. A critical part of such systems is the word-level translation model, which is estimated from aligned data. Currently, the standard way of computing a word alignment is to estimate a function linking words in one of the languages to words in the other. Functions can only define many-to-one relations, but word alignment is a many-to-many relation. The solution is to combine two functions, one in each direction, and harmonize them by means of some heuristic. After that, phrases can be extracted from the word alignments.

The problem is that the starting point for word alignments is usually the IBM models (Brown *et al.*, 1993), which are known to produce flawed alignments, in large part because they (1) model reordering by allowing unrestricted movement of words, rather than constrained movement of compositional units, and therefore must (2) attempt to compensate via directed, asymmetric distortion and fertility models.

Proceedings of SSST-3, Third Workshop on Syntax and Structure in Statistical Translation, pages 28–36,
Boulder, Colorado, June 2009.

The conventional heuristics for attempting to recover from the resulting alignment errors is to estimate two directed models in opposite directions and then intersect their alignments – to make up for the fact that, in reality, word alignment is an inherently joint relation. It is unfortunate that such a critical stage in the training process of an SMT system relies on inaccurate heuristics, which have been largely motivated by historical implementation factors, rather than principles explaining language phenomena.

Inversion Transduction Grammar (ITG) models provide a natural, alternative approach, by estimating the joint word alignment relation directly, eliminating the need for any of the conventional heuristics. A transduction grammar is a grammar that generates sentences in two languages (L_0 and L_1) simultaneously; i.e., one start symbol expands into two strings, as for example in Figure 1(b). A transduction grammar explains two languages simultaneously. ITGs model a class of transductions (sets of sentence translations) with expressive power and computational complexity falling between (a) finite-state transducers or FSTs and (b) syntax-directed transduction grammars[1] or SDTGs. An ITG produces both a common structural form for a sentence pairs, as well as relating the words – aligning them. This could actually work as the joint word alignment that is usually constructed by heuristic function combination.

Yet despite the substantial body of literature on word alignment, ITG based models, and phrase-based SMT, the existing work has not assessed the potential for improving phrase-based translation quality by using joint ITG based word alignments to replace the error-prone conditional IBM model based word alignments and associated heuristics for intersecting bidirectional IBM alignments.

On one hand, word alignment work is usually evaluated not on actual translation quality, but rather on artificial metrics like alignment error rate (AER, Och & Ney, 2003), which relies on a manually annotated gold standard word alignment. There are some indications that ITG produces better alignment then the standard method (Zhao & Vogel, 2003, Zhang & Gildea 2005, Chao & Li, 2007). There is, however, little inherent utility in alignments – their value is determined by the SMT systems one can build from them. In fact, recent studies have discredited the earlier assumption that lower AER is correlated with improved translation quality – the opposite can very well occur (Ayan & Dorr, 2006). Therefore it is essential to evaluate the quality of the word alignment not in terms of AER, but rather in terms of actual translation quality in a system built from it.

On the other hand, ITG models have been employed to improve translation quality as measured by BLEU (Papineni *et al.*, 2002), but still without directly addressing the problem of dependence on inaccurate IBM alignments. Sánchez & Benedí (2006) construct an ITG from word alignments computed by the conventional IBM model, which does little to alleviate the problems. Sima'an & Mylonakis (2008) use an ITG to structure a prior distribution to a phrase extraction system, which is an altogether different approach. Cherry & Lin (2007) do use ITG to build word alignments, but blur the lines by still mixing in the conventional IBM method, and focus on phrase extraction.

The present work clearly demonstrates, for the first time to our knowledge, that replacing the widely-used heuristic of intersecting IBM word alignments from two directed conditional models instead with a single ITG alignment from a joint model produces superior translation accuracy. The experiments are performed on three distinct language pairs: German–English, Spanish–English, and French–English. Translation accuracy is reported in terms of BLEU, NIST, and METEOR metrics.

2 Background

Statistical Machine Translation is a paradigm where translation is considered as a code-breaking problem. The goal is to find the most likely output sentence (clear text message) given the supplied input sentence (coded message), according to some model.

To get a probabilistic model, large amounts of training data are used. These data have to be aligned so that an understanding of correspondences between the languages is there to be learnt from. Even if the data is assumed to be aligned at sentence level, sub-sentence alignment is also needed. This is usually carried out by training some statistical model of a word-to-word function (Brown *et al.*, 1993), or a hidden Markov model consuming input words and emitting output words

[1] Which "synchronous CFGs" are essentially identical to.

(Vogel, Ney & Tillmann, 1996). The toolkit GIZA++ (Och & Ney, 2000) is freely available and widely used to compute such word alignments.

All these models learn a directed translation function that maps input words to output words. Since these functions focus solely on surface phenomena, they have no mechanisms for dealing with the kind of structured reordering between languages that could account for, e.g., the difference between SVO languages and SOV languages.

What emerges is in fact a rather flawed model of how one language is rewritten into another. The conventional way to alleviate this flaw is to train an equally flawed model in the other direction, and then intersect the two. This practice certainly alleviates some of the problems, but far from all.

To build a phrase-based SMT system, the word alignment is used as a starting point to try to account for the entire sentence. This means that the word alignment is gradually expanded, so that all words in both sentences are accounted for, either by words in the other language, or by the *null* empty word ε. This process is called grow-diag-final (Koehn, Och & Marcu, 2003).

The grow-diag-final process does smooth over some of the flaws still left in the word alignment, but error analysis gives reason to doubt that it repairs enough of the errors to avoid damaging translation accuracy. Thus, we are motivated to investigate a completely different approach that attempts to avoid the noisy directed alignments in the first place.

2.1 Inversion Transduction Grammars

A **transduction** is a set of sentence translation pairs – just as a language is a set of sentences. The set defines a relation between the input and output languages.

In the *generative* view, a **transduction grammar** generates a transduction, i.e., a set of sentence translation pairs or **bisentences** – just as an ordinary (monolingual) language grammar generates a language, i.e., a set of sentences. In the *recognition* view, alternatively, a transduction grammar **biparses** or accepts all sentence pairs of a transduction – just as a language grammar parses or accepts all sentences of a language. And in the *transduction* view, a transduction grammar **transduces** (translates) input sentences to output sentences.

Two familiar classes of transductions have been in widespread use for decades in many areas of computer science and linguistics:

> A **syntax-directed transduction** is a set of bisentences generated by some **syntax-directed transduction grammar** or SDTG (Lewis & Stearns, 1968; Aho & Ullman, 1969, 1972). A "synchronous CFG" is equivalent to an SDTG.

> A **finite-state transduction** is a set of bisentences generated by some **finite-state transducer** or FST. It is possible to describe finite-state transductions using SDTGs (or synchronous CFGs) by restricting them alternatively to the special cases of either "right regular SDTGs" or "left regular SDTGs". However, such characterizations rather misleadingly overlook the key point – by severely limiting expressive power, finite-state transductions are orders of magnitude cheaper to biparse, train, and induce than syntax-directed transductions – and are often even more accurate to induce.

More recently, an intermediate equivalence class of transductions whose generative capacity and computational complexity falls in between these two has become widely used in state-of-the-art MT systems – due to numerous empirical results indicating significantly better fit to modeling translation between many human language pairs:

> An **inversion transduction** is a set of bisentences generated by some **inversion transduction grammar** or ITG (Wu, 1995a, 1995b, 1997). As above with finite-state transductions, it is possible to describe inversion transductions using SDTGs (or synchronous CFGs) by restricting them alternatively to the special cases of "binary SDTGs", "ternary SDTGs", or "SDTGs whose transduction rules are restricted to straight and inverted permutations only". Again however, as above, such characterizations rather misleadingly overlook the key point – by severely limiting expressive power, inversion transductions are orders of magnitude cheaper to biparse, train, and induce than syntax-directed transductions – and are often even more accurate to induce.

Any SDTG (or synchronous CFG) of binary rank – i.e., that has at most two nonterminals on the right-hand-side of any rule – is an ITG. (Similarly, any SDTG (or synchronous CFG) that is right regular is a finite-state transduction grammar.) Thus, for example, any grammar computed by the binarization algorithm of Zhang *et al.*

(2006) is an ITG. Similarly, any grammar induced following the hierarchical phrase-based translation method, which always yields a binary transduction grammar (Chiang 2005), is an ITG.

Moreover, any SDTG (or synchronous CFG) of ternary rank – i.e., that has at most three nonterminals on the right-hand-side of any rule – is still equivalent to an ITG. Of course, this does not hold for SDTGs (or synchronous CFGs) in general, which allow arbitrary rank (possibly exceeding three) at the price of exponential complexity, as summarized in Table 1.

monolingual		*bilingual*	
regular or finite-state languages **FSA** *or* *CFG that is right regular or left regular*	$O(n^2)$	regular or finite-state transductions **FST** *or* *SDTG (or synchronous CFG) that is right regular or left regular*	$O(n^4)$
context-free languages **CFG**	$O(n^3)$	inversion transductions **ITG** *or* *SDTG (or synchronous CFG) that is binary or ternary or inverting*	$O(n^6)$
		syntax-directed transductions **SDTG** *(or synchronous CFG)*	$O(n^{2n+2})$

Table 1: Summary comparison of computational complexity for Viterbi and chart (bi)parsing, and EM training algorithms for both monolingual and bilingual hierarchies.

Without loss of generality, any ITG can be conveniently written in a **2-normal form** (Wu, 1995a, 1997). This cannot be done for SDTGs (or synchronous CFGs) – unlike the monolingual case of CFGs, which form an equivalence class of context-free languages that can all be written in Chomsky's 2-normal form. In the bilingual case, only ITGs form an equivalence class of inversion transductions that can all be written in a 2-normal form.

Formally, an ITG in this 2-normal form, which segregates syntactic versus lexical rules, consists of a tuple $\langle N, V_0, V_1, R, S \rangle$ where N is a set of nonterminal symbols, V_0 and V_1 are the vocabularies of L_0 and L_1 respectively, R is a set of transduction rules, and $S \in N$ is the start symbol. Each **transduction rule** takes one of the following forms:

```
S → X
X → [Y Z]
X → <Y Z>
X → segment_L0/ε
X → ε/segment_L1
X → segment_L0/segment_L1
```

where `X`, `Y` and `Z` may be any nonterminal.

Aside from the start rule, there are two kinds of **syntactic transduction rules**, namely **straight** and **inverted**. In the above notation, straight transduction rules `X → [Y Z]` use square brackets, whereas inverted rules `X → <Y Z>` use angled brackets. The transductions generated by straight nodes have the same order in both languages, whereas the transduction generated by the inverted nodes are inverted in one of the languages, meaning that the children are read left-to-right in L_0 and right-to-left in L_1. In Figure 1(b) for example, the parse tree node instantiating an inverted transduction rule is marked with a horizontal bar. This mechanism allows for a minimal amount of reordering, while keeping the complexity down.

The last three forms are for **lexical transduction rules**. Each `segment` comes from the vocabulary of one of the languages, indicated by the subscript. In the simplest case, the two ε-rule forms define **singletons**, which insert "spurious" segments into either language. Spurious segments lack any correspondence in the other language – they are "aligned to *null*" – and singletons are lexical rules that associate a *null*-aligned segment in one of the languages with an empty segment (ε) in the other.

On the other hand, the last rule form defines a **lexical translation pair** that aligns the word/phrase `segment`$_{L0}$ to its translation `segment`$_{L1}$. Such rules can also be written compositionally as a pair of singletons, although it reads less transparently:

```
X → segment_L0/ε ε/segment_L1
```

Note that **segments** typically consist of multiple **tokens**. Common examples include:

- Chinese word/phrase segments consisting of multiple unsegmented character tokens
- Chinese word/phrase segments consisting of multiple smaller, presegmented multi-character word/phrase tokens
- English phrase/collocation segments consisting of multiple word tokens (*roller coaster*)

ITGs inherently model phrasal translation – linguistically speaking, ITGs assume the set of lexical translation pairs constitutes a **phrasal lexicon** (just as lexicographers assume in building ordinary everyday dictionaries). An advantage of this is that the ITG biparsing and decoding algorithms perform integrated **translation-driven segmentation** simultaneously with optimizing the parse (Wu, 1997; Wu & Wong, 1998).

These properties allow an ITG to (1) insert and delete words/phrases, which matches the ability of the conventional methods for word alignment as well as phrase alignment, and (2) account for the reordering in a more principled and restricted way than conventional alignment methods.

A **stochastic ITG** or SITG is an ITG where every rule is associated with a probability. As with a stochastic CFG (SCFG), the probabilities are conditioned on the left-hand-side symbol, so that the probability of rule $X \rightarrow \chi$ is $p(\chi|X)$.

A **bracketing ITG** or BITG or BTG (Wu, 1995a) contains only one nonterminal symbol, with syntactic transduction rules `X → [X X]` and `X → <X X>`, which means that it produces a bracketing rather than a labeled tree. With a **stochastic BITG** (SBITG or SBTG) it is still possible to determine an optimal tree, since inversion and alignment are coupled: where inversions are needed is decided by the translations, and vice versa.

In Wu (1995b) algorithms for training a SITG using expectation maximization, as well as finding the optimal parse of a sentence pair given a SITG are presented. These are polynomial time $O(n^6)$, as seen in Table 1. Further pruning methods can also be added, especially for longer sentences.

2.2 Previous uses of ITG in alignment

There have been several attempts to use various forms of ITGs in an alignment setting.

Zhao & Vogel (2003) and Sánchez & Benedí (2006) both use GIZA++ to establish their SITG. Since they use GIZA++ to create their ITG, little light is shed on the question of whether an ITG produces better alignments than GIZA++.

Zhang & Gildea (2005) compare lexicalized and standard ITGs on an alignment task, and conclude that both are superior to IBM models 1 and 4, and that lexicalization helps. They also employ some pruning techniques to speed up training. Chao & Li (2007) incorporate the reordering constraints imposed by an ITG to their discriminative word aligner, and also note a lower alignment error rate in their system. Since neither work evaluates results on a translation task, it is hard to know whether better AER would translate into improved translation quality, in light of Ayan & Dorr (2006).

Sima'an & Mylonakis (2008) use an ITG as the basis of a prior distribution in their system that extracts all possible phrases rather than employing a length cut-off, and report an increase in translation quality as measured by the BLEU score (Papineni *et al.*, 2002). In this paper, it is not primarily pure ITG that is being evaluated, but it lends some credibility to our assumption that the ITG structure helps when aligning.

Cherry & Lin (2007) use an ITG to produce phrase tables that are then used in a translation system. However, to make their system outperform GIZA++, they blend in a non-compositionality constraint that is still based on GIZA++ word alignments. We would very much like to clearly see and understand the difference between ITG and GIZA++ alignments, and the lines are somewhat blurred in their work.

3 Model

First, the lexicon of the SBITG is initialized, by extracting lexical transduction rules from cooccurrence data from the corpus. Each pair of tokens in each sentence pair is initially considered equally likely to be a lexical translation pair. Each token is also considered to be a possible singleton. The two syntactic transduction rules `X → [X X]` and `X → <X X>` are initially assumed to be equally likely.

Then full expectation-maximization training (Wu, 1995b) is carried out on the training data. Instead of waiting for full convergence, the process is halted when the increase in the training data's probability starts to decline.

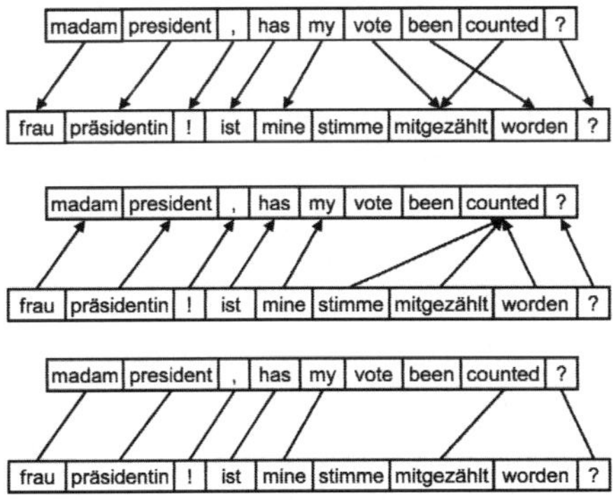

(a)

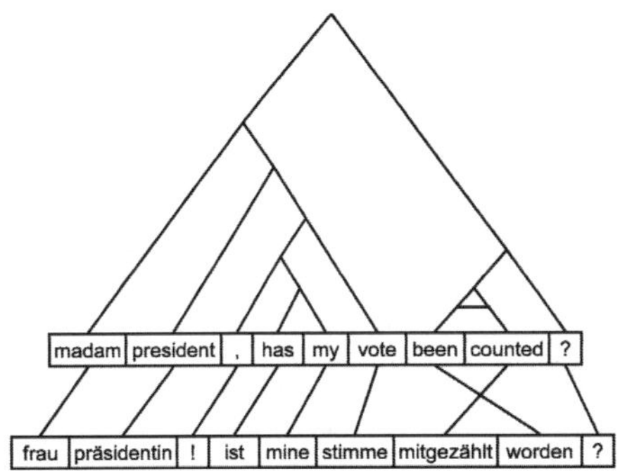

(b)

Figure 1: (a) Bidirectional IBM alignments and their intersection and (b) ITG alignments.

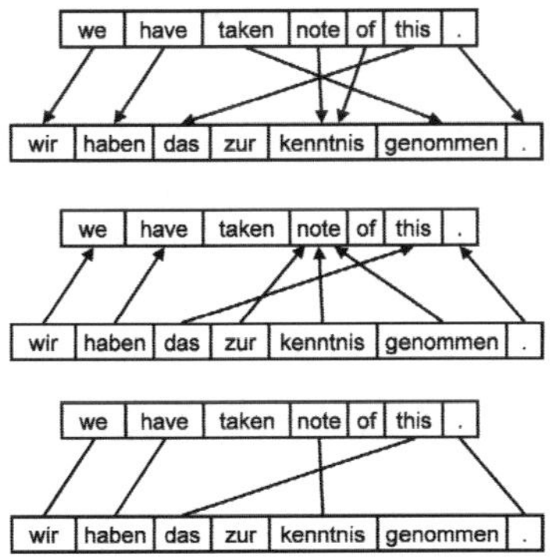

(a)

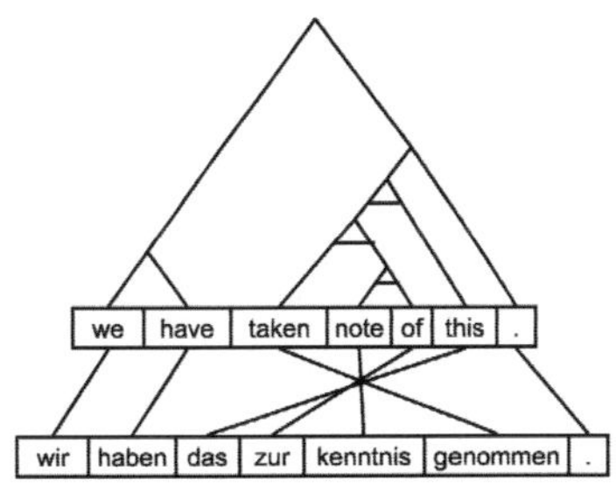

(b)

Figure 2: (a) Bidirectional IBM alignments and their intersection and (b) ITG alignments.

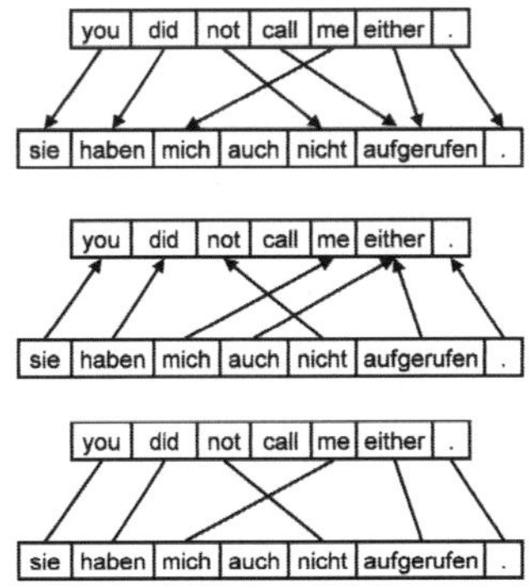

(a)

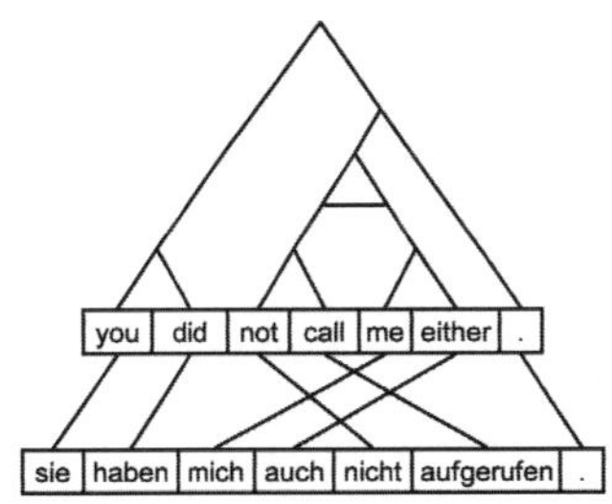

(b)

Figure 3: (a) Bidirectional IBM alignments and their intersection and (b) ITG alignments.

At this point, we extract the optimal parses from the training data, and use the word alignment imposed by the ITG instead of the one computed by GIZA++ (Och & Ney, 2000). Training after this point is carried out according to the guidelines for the WSMT08 baseline system (see section 4.2). In Figure 1(a) is an example of a sentence aligned with GIZA++, and in Figure 1(b) is the same sentence, aligned with ITG. In this case it is clearly visible how the structured reordering constraints that the ITG enforces results in a clear alignment, whereas GIZA++ is unable to sort it out.

	sentence pairs	tokens
de-en	115,323	1,602,781
es-en	108,073	1,466,132
fr-en	95,990	1,340,718

Table 2: Summary of training data.

4 Experimental setup

4.1 Data

We used a subset of the data provided for the Second Workshop on Statistical Machine Translation[2], which consists mainly of texts from the Europarl corpus (Koehn, 2005). We used the Europarl part for the translation tasks: German–English (de-en), Spanish–English (es-en), and French–English (fr-en). Table 2 summarizes the datasets used for training. For tuning and testing, the tuning and development test sets provided for the workshop were used – each measuring 2,000 sentence pairs.

4.2 Baseline system

For baseline system we trained phrase-based SMT models with GIZA++ (Och & Ney, 2000), the training scripts supplied with Moses (Koehn *et al.*,

[2] *www.statmt.org/wmt08*

2007), and minimum error rate training (MERT, Och, 2003), all according to the WSMT08-guidelines for baseline systems. This means that 5 iterations are carried out with IBM model 1 training, 5 iterations with HMM training, 3 iterations of IBM model 3 training, and finally 3 iterations of IBM model 4 training. After GIZA++ training, the Moses training script extracts and scores phrases, and establishes a lexicalized reordering model.

The WSMT08 guidelines call for the combination heuristic "grow-diag-final-and" (GDFA). We also tried the "intersect" combination heuristic, which simply calculates the intersection of alignment points in the two directed alignments provided by GIZA++.

4.3 SBITG system

Since imposing an SBITG biparse on a sentence pair forces a word alignment on the sentence pair, word alignment under SBITG models is identical to biparsing.

Expectation-maximization training was used to induce a SBITG from the training data. Training is halted when the EM-process started to converge. In our experience, convergence typically requires no more than 3 iterations or so. When EM training is finished, we extracted the optimal biparses from the training data, which then constitute the optimal alignment given the grammar. This alignment was then output in GIZA++ format. All singletons from the SBITG alignment were converted to be *null*-alignments in the GIZA++ formatted file. These files could then be used instead of GIZA++ in the remainder of the training process for the phrase-based translation system.

Although the results from the ITG are interpreted as two directed alignments, they are identical, both with each other and the intersection. Trying different combination heuristics for these results always yields the same results.

The training process was identical save for the fact that the word alignments were produced by SBITGs rather than by GIZA++.

5 Experimental results

We trained a total of nine systems (three tasks and three different alignments), which we evaluated with three different measures: BLEU (Papineni *et al.*, 2002), NIST (Doddington, 2002), and METEOR (Lavie & Agarwal 2007).

Figure 2 shows a sentence pair as it was aligned with the two different models. Figure 2(a) shows the GIZA++ alignment in both directions, and the intersection between them, whereas Figure 2(b) shows the SBITG alignment with its common structure. The asymmetric reordering mechanism of the IBM models is simply unable to relate the two halves to one another. The segment *zur kenntnis genommen* could certainly be said to mean *note*, but as a verb, and not as a noun, which is the current usage of the word. This is an inherent problem of the asymmetry of the IBM models, which is rectified by simultaneous alignment.

Figure 3 shows another sentence pair. Again, Figure 3(a) was aligned with GIZA++ and Figure 3(b) with the SITG model. This shows a case with perhaps even more structured reordering, where a notion of constituency is definitely needed to get it right. SITG handles constituency, and gets this issue right. The IBM models do not, resulting in the error of aligning *either* to *aufgerufen*.

As mentioned before, the GDFA heuristic is applied after the word alignment process, and it does fix some of these problems. Therefore we opted to evaluate this, not on alignments, but rather on translation quality of phrase based SMT systems derived from the alignments. Our empirical results confirm that SBITG alignments do indeed lead to better translation quality, as shown in Table 2.

We also tried the intersect combination heuristic, and depending on language pair and evaluation metric, the GDFA and intersect heuristics come out on top. The ITG approach is, however, consistently better than either of the heuristics applied to GIZA++ output.

6 Discussion

There are of course fundamental differences between ITG and IBM models. The main difference is that IBM models are directed and surface oriented, whereas the ITG model is joint and structured. The directedness means that the IBM models are unable to produce a word alignment that is optimal for a sentence pair; they can only produce word alignments that are optimal when translating from one language into the other. An ITG on the other hand is capable of producing the optimal alignment that explains both sentences in the pair. We see this phenomenon clearly in Figures 1–3.

	BLEU			NIST			METEOR		
	GIZA++		SBITG	GIZA++		SBITG	GIZA++		SBITG
	GDFA	inters.		GDFA	inters.		GDFA	inters.	
de-en	20.59	20.69	**21.13**	5.8668	5.8623	**5.9380**	0.4969	0.4953	**0.5029**
es-en	25.97	26.33	**26.63**	6.6352	6.6793	**6.7407**	0.5599	0.5582	**0.5612**
fr-en	26.03	26.17	**26.63**	6.6907	6.7071	**6.8151**	0.5544	0.5560	**0.5635**

Table 2: Results. The best result on each task/metric combination is in bold digits. (The identical results for SBITG on Spanish–English and French–English are not typos.)

IBM models are also built to allow for fairly "whimsical" reorderings, which are not modeled very well to begin with. This allows for far too many degrees of freedom to fit the model to the data. Because natural languages are inherently structural, this excess degree of freedom could hurt performance. Some restraints are needed. ITGs on the other hand only allow for compositionally structured reordering, which corresponds better to the reorderings between natural languages. There are some issues with ITG as well, one of them being that all permutations are actually not allowed, even if structured. This has led to some problems when an a prior alignment or structure is forced upon a sentence pair, but using unrestricted expectation-maximization means that the sentence pair is fitted to the grammar, and what the grammar cannot express is not applied to the data. Even if ITG proves to be too restrictive in the future, the fact that it bases reordering on structure, rather than unrestricted lexical movement, gives it an edge over the IBM models. The benefits of structured reordering as opposed to unrestricted are clearly visible in Figures 1–3.

An argument to continue using IBM models is that two directed alignments can be intersected and heuristically grown to build a joint alignment, thus compensating for the flaws in the original models. But as we have seen in Figure 3, even the combination of two models contains errors that should have been avoided. This approach is not able to smooth over the flaws of the IBM models.

The results in this paper give credibility to the claim that these limitations of the IBM models are so serious that they hurt translation quality of systems built upon them; even after the phrase building heuristic has been applied. Systems built on ITG alignment on the other hand fare better, on all three evaluation metrics.

There is still more to be done. So far we have only employed bracketing SITGs, which are not able to distinguish one structure form another. The structural changes that the SBITG is capable of are dictated by the alignment of the leaves in the tree. This seems impressive, given the information at hand, but is really a logical conclusion of the fact that the grammar can leverage different alignment probabilities against each other, and as the alignment is coupled to the structure of the ITG parse, the structure is constrained to the alignment. The reverse is also true: the alignment is constrained by the structure. This coupling is essential to the training of SITGs. For a SBITG, there is very little information in the structure, only the decision to read the node as straight or inverted. This is not an inherent property of ITGs in general; more information can be carried higher up in the tree by labeling the nonterminals. There is great hope that adding more information to the structuring, even better alignments could be gained.

In this paper we have extracted the word alignments from ITG biparses, and inserted them into the conventional phrase-based SMT pipeline. It is feasible to extract phrases directly from the grammar, as demonstrated by Cherry & Lin (2007). Our results suggest that augmenting other portions of the phrase-based SMT framework with ITG structures might also be worth exploring, in particular decoding. Recall that in the transduction view of transduction grammars (as opposed to generative or recognition views), an output translation can be determined by parsing an input sentence with a transduction grammar (Wu 1996; Wu & Wong 1998). This kind of translation would also entail the notion of structure that we have just witnessed helping alignment. Phrase-based SMT currently relies on unrestricted phrasal movement, which is a lot better than unrestricted lexical movement, but could probably use some structure as well.

7 Conclusion

We have shown that learning word alignments through a compositionally-structured, joint process yields higher phrase-based translation accuracy than the conventional heuristic of intersecting conditional models.

The conventional method with IBM-models suffers from their directionality. The asymmetry causes bad alignments. We have instead introduced an automatically induced ITG alignment that does not suffer from this asymmetry, and is able to explain the two sentences simultaneously rather than one in terms of the other. The IBM-models also suffers from a simplified reordering model, which relies on moving individual words. The hierarchical structure of ITGs means that even a BITG has enough structural information to outperform the IBM models. Previous work shows that these advantages translate into better alignments as measured against a manually annotated gold standard using alignment error rate (AER). Previous work also shows that AER is a poor indicator of whether translation quality is increased. We have showed that the increase in alignment quality actually translates into an increase in translation quality in this case, as measured by BLEU, NIST and METEOR across three different language pairs.

Acknowledgments

This material is based upon work supported in part by the Swedish National Graduate School of Language Technology, the Olof Gjerdmans Travel Grant, the Defense Advanced Research Projects Agency (DARPA) under GALE Contract No. HR0011-06-C-0023, and the Hong Kong Research Grants Council (RGC) under research grants GRF621008, DAG03/04.EG09, RGC6256/00E, and RGC6083/99E. Any opinions, findings and conclusions or recommendations expressed in this material are those of the authors and do not necessarily reflect the views of the Defense Advanced Research Projects Agency.

References

AHO, Alfred V. & Jeffrey D. ULLMAN (1969) "Syntax-directed translations and the pushdown assembler" in *Journal of Computer and System Sciences* **3**: 37–56.

AHO, Alfred V. & Jeffrey D. ULLMAN (1972) *The Theory of Parsing, Translation, and Compiling* (Volumes 1 and 2). Englewood Cliffs, NJ: Prentice-Hall.

AYAN, Necip Fazil & Bonnie J. DORR (2006) "Going Beyond AER: An Extensive Analysis of Word Alignments and Their Impact on MT" in *COLING-ACL '06*, pp. 9–16, Sydney, Australia, July 2006.

BROWN, Peter F., Stephen A. DELLA PIETRA, Vincent J. DELLA PIETRA & Robert L. MERCER (1993) "The Mathematics of Statistical Machine Translation" in *Computational Linguistics* **19**(2): 263–311.

CHAO, Wen-Han & Zhou-Jun LI (2007) "Incorporating Constituent Structure Constraint into Discriminative Word Alignment" in *MT Summit XI*, pp. 97–103, Copenhagen, Denmark.

CHERRY, Colin & Dekang LIN (2007) "Inversion Transduction Grammar for Joint Phrasal Translation Modeling" in *Proceedings of SSST*, pp. 17–24, Rochester, New York, April 2007.

CHIANG, David (2005) "A Hierarchical Phrase-Based Model for Statistical Machine Translation" in *ACL-2005*, pp. 263–270, Ann Arbor, MI, June 2005.

KOEHN, Philipp, Franz Josef OCH & Daniel MARCU (2003) "Statistical Phrase-based Translation" in *HLT-NAACL '03*, pp. 127–133.

KOEHN, Philipp (2005) "Europarl: A Parallel Corpus for Statistical Machine Translation" in *MT Summit X*, Phuket, Thailand, September 2005.

DODDINGTON, George (2002) "Automatic Evaluation of Machine Translation Quality using n-gram Co-occurrence Statistics" in *HLT-2002*. San Diego, California.

KOEHN, Philipp, Hieu HOANG, Alexandra BIRCH, Chris CALLISON-BURCH, Marcello FEDERICO, Nicola BERTOLDI, Brooke COWAN, Wade SHEN, Christine MORAN, Richard ZENS, Chris DYER, Ondrej BOJAR, Alexandra CONSTANTIN & Evan HERBST (2007) "Moses: Open Source Toolkit for Statistical Machine Translation" in *ACL '07*, Prague, Czech Republic, June 2007.

LAVIE, Alon & Abhaya AGARWAL (2007) "METEOR: An Automatic Metric for MT Evaluation with High Levels of Correlation with Human Judgment" in *WSMT*. Prague, Czech Republic, June 2007.

LEWIS, Philip M. & Richard E. STEARNS. (1968) "Syntax-directed transduction" in *Journal of the ACM* **15**: 465–488.

OCH, Franz Josef & Hermann NEY (2000) "Improved Statistical Alignment Models" in *ACL-2000*, pp. 440–447, Hong Kong, October 2000.

OCH, Franz Josef (2003) "Minimum error rate training in statistical machine translation" in *ACL '03*.

OCH, Franz Josef & Hermann NEY (2003) "A Systematic Comparison of Various Statistical Alignment Models" in *Computational Linguistics* 29(1), pp. 19–52.

PAPINENI, Kishore, Salim ROUKOS, Todd WARD & Wei-Jing ZHU (2002) "BLEU: a Method for Automatic Evaluation of Machine Translation" in *ACL '02*, pp 311-318. Philadelphia, Pennsylvania.

SÁNCHEZ, J. A., J.M. BENEDÍ (2006) "Stochastic Inversion Transduction Grammars for Obtaining Word Phrases for Phrase-based Statistical Machine Translation" in *WSMT*, pp. 130–133, New York City, June 2006.

SIMA'AN, Khalil & Markos MYLONAKIS (2008) "Better Statistical Estimation Can Benefit all Phrases in Phrase-based Statistical Machine Translation" in *SLT 2008*, pp. 237–240, Goa, India, December 2008.

VOGEL, Stephan, Hermann NEY & Christoph TILLMANN (1996) "HMM-based Word Alignment in Statistical Translation" in *COLING '96*, pp. 836–841.

WU, Dekai (1995a) "An Algorithm for Simultaneously Bracketing Parallel Texts by Aligning Words" in *ACL '95*, pp. 244–251, Cambridge, Massachusetts, June 1995.

WU, Dekai (1995b) "Trainable Coarse Bilingual Grammars for Parallel Text Bracketing" in *WVLC-3*, pp. 69–82, Cambridge, Massachusetts, June 1995.

WU, Dekai (1996) "A polynomial-time algorithm for statistical machine translation" in *ACL-96*, Santa Cruz, CA: June 1996.

WU, Dekai (1997) "Stochastic Inversion Transduction Grammars and Bilingual Parsing of Parallel Corpora" in *Computational Linguistics* 23(3), pp 377–403.

WU, Dekai & Hongsing WONG (1998) "Machine Translation with a Stochastic Grammatical Channel" in *COLING-ACL'98*, Montreal, August 1998.

ZHANG, Hao & Daniel GILDEA (2005) "Stochastic Lexicalized Inversion Transduction Grammar for Alignment" in *ACL '05*, pp. 475–482, Ann Arbor, June 2005.

ZHANG, Hao, Liang HUANG, Dan GILDEA & Kevin KNIGHT (2006) "Synchronous Binarization for Machine Translation" in *HLT/NAACL-2006*, pp. 256–263, New York, June 2006.

ZHAO, Bing & Stephan VOGEL (2003) "Word Alignment Based on Bilingual Bracketing" in *HLT-NAACL Workshop: Building and Using Parallel Texts*, pp. 15–18, Edmonton, May–June 2003.

References Extension for the Automatic Evaluation of MT by Syntactic Hybridization

Bo Wang, Tiejun Zhao, Muyun Yang, Sheng Li
School of Computer Science and Technology
Harbin Institute of Technology
Harbin, China
{bowang,tjzhao,ymy,sl}@mtlab.hit.edu.cn

Abstract

Because of the variations of the languages, the coverage of the references is very important to the reference based automatic evaluation of machine translation systems. We propose a method to extend the reference set of the automatic evaluation only based on multiple manual references and their syntactic structures. In our approach, the syntactic equivalents in the reference sentences are identified and hybridized to generate new references. The new method need no external knowledge and can obtain the equivalents of long sub-segments of reference sentences. The experimental results show that using the extended reference set the popular automatic evaluation metrics achieve better correlations with the human assessments.

1 Introduction

While human evaluation of machine translation output remains the most reliable method to assess translation quality, it is a costly and time consuming process. The development of automatic machine translation evaluation metrics enables the rapid assessment of system output. By providing immediate feedback on the effectiveness of various techniques, these metrics have guided machine translation research and have facilitated rapid advances in the state of the art. In addition, automatic evaluation metrics are useful in comparing the performance of multiple machine translation systems on a given translation task. Since automatic evaluation metrics are meant to serve as a surrogate for human judgments, their quality is determined by how well they correlate with assessors' preferences and how accurately they predicts human judgments.

Although current methods for automatically evaluating machine translation output do not require humans to assess individual system output, humans are nevertheless needed to generate a number of reference translations. The quality of machine-generated translations is determined by automatically comparing system output with these references. All current automatic evaluation metrics are based on the various measures of the general similarity between the system translation and manual references. This kind of method has an obvious drawback: it does not account for combinations of lexical and syntactic differences that might occur between a perfectly fluent and accurately-translated machine output and a human reference translation (beyond variations already captured by the different reference translations themselves). Moreover, the set of human reference translations is unlikely to be an exhaustive inventory of "good translations" for any given foreign language sentence. Therefore, it would be highly desirable to extend the coverage of the references for the similarity based evaluation methods.

To match the system translation with various presentation of the same meaning, many work haven been proposed to extend the references by generating lexical variations. The first strategy focuses on the extension based on paraphrase identi-

Proceedings of SSST-3, Third Workshop on Syntax and Structure in Statistical Translation, pages 37–44,
Boulder, Colorado, June 2009.

fication (Lepage and Denoual, 2005; Lassner et al. 2005; Zhou et al. 2006; Kauchak and Barzilay, 2006; Owczarzak et al. 2006; Owczarzak et al. 2007). In this kind of method, the quality of system translations can be viewed as the extent to which the conveyed meaning matches the semantics of the reference translations, independent of substrings they may share. In short, all paraphrases of human-generated references should be considered "good" translations. The second strategy extends the references with the synonymy (Banerjee and Lavie, 2005; Lassner et al. 2005). This is an alternation to obtain lexical variations with synonymy dictionaries instead of the paraphrase. In this kind of method, the reference is matched against to the system translation with the pack of the synonymies of the reference words instead of the exact matching.

Both two strategies can successfully capture the lexical variations and greatly extend the coverage of the references. But they still have two common deficiencies. The first is the demand of the external knowledge. Paraphrase based method need a mass of external corpus to extract paraphrases and synonymy based method need manually constructed semantic dictionaries. These demands seriously limit the application on various languages for which the external knowledge is absent.

Another deficiency is that the two strategies cannot capture the equivalents of long sub-segments such as a clause. Synonymy based method can only capture the equivalents of single words. Paraphrase based method can capture the equivalents of longer units but the length is still very narrow. In many cases, some long sub-segments can be varied with an entirely different presentation which cannot be decomposed into the variations of words or phrases.

To address these problems we propose a novel strategy to generate variations presentation only using existing multiple manual references without any external knowledge. We identify the syntactic components on different level as the replaceable units and determine the syntactic equivalents of the components in the corresponding references. Then the equivalents of the syntactic components are hybridized into new references.

The rest of the paper is organized as follows. Section 2 introduces the concept and identification of the syntactic equivalents. Section 3 proposes a process to hybridize the syntactic equivalents efficiently. Experimental results are illustrated in section 4. We also include some related discussion in Section 5. Finally this work is concluded in Section 6.

2 Syntactic Equivalents

In our approach, we propose a novel method to obtain the equivalents of the sub-segments from the corresponding references to a single source sentence. A sub-segment can be a word, a phrase or longer unit such as a clause. As we know, the variations of the sentences to the same meaning can be distinguished into two categories. The first is the structural variations. In this case, presentations employ the same words but arrange them in different structure. The second is lexical variations. In this case, presentations have the same structure but employ the different words. In practice, one reference sentence often has both of the two kinds of variations comparing with other corresponding reference sentences.

As the previous works, we also focus on the lexical variations. The approach is that the equivalents of the words are not obtained by external knowledge. In our strategy, generally speaking, the equivalents of a sub-segment S in a reference sentence are identified as the sub-segments which play the same syntactic role in the same structure in the other corresponding references. The equivalents obtained in this way are called syntactic equivalents.

Suppose R_1 and R_2 is a corresponding reference sentence pair. T_1 and T_2 are the consecutive syntactic trees of R_1 and R_2 respectively. We formally define a syntactic equivalent pair between R_1 and R_2 with a 4-tuple:

$$<N_1, N_2, S_1, S_2>$$

where N_i is a non-terminal node in T_i and S_i is the sub-segment which is covered by N_i. Then, all the syntactic equivalent pair R_1 and R_2 can be recursively identified using following process:

- The first syntactic equivalent pair $<N_1, N_2, S_1, S_2>$ is identified where N_i is the root of T_i and $S_i = R_i$.
- Suppose $<N_1, N_2, S_1, S_2>$ is a syntactic equivalent pair. $\{N_{11}, N_{12}, \ldots N_{1m}\}$ and $\{N_{21}, N_{22}, \ldots N_{2n}\}$ are the child nodes sequences of

N_1 and N_2 respectively. If $n=m$ and $N_{1i}= N_{2i}$ (i.e. the child nodes sequence of N_1 and N_2 are exactly the same), for each node pair N_{1i} and N_{2i} a syntactic equivalent pair is identified as $< N_{1i}, N_{2i}, S_{1i}, S_{2i}>$.

With this process, all equivalent pairs on different syntactic level can be identified by synchronously traveling the two trees from top to bottom. The following is an example of the identification of the equivalent pairs. Figure 1 gives out a reference sentence pair and their syntactic trees. The nodes which are included in certain equivalent pair are surrounded by a rectangle.

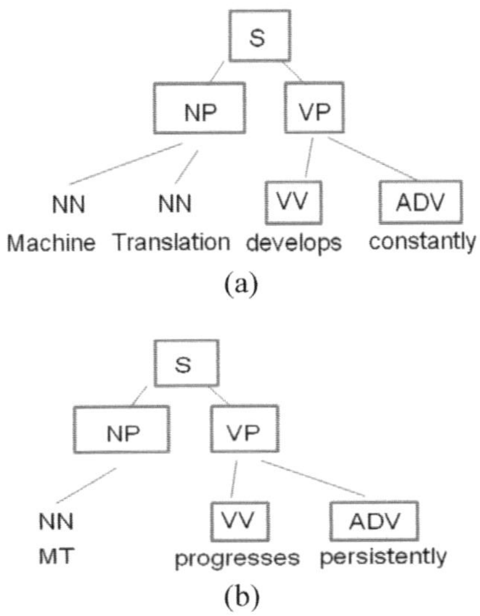

Figure 1 An example of the identification of the syntactic equivalent pairs.

In this example, five equivalent pairs can be identified:

- *<S, S, "Machine translation develops constantly", "MT progresses persistently">*
- *<NP, NP, "Machine translation", "MT">*
- *<VP, VP, "develops constantly", "progresses persistently">*
- *<VV, VV, "develops", "progresses">*
- *<ADV, ADV, "constantly", "persistently">*

3 Hybridization of Syntactic Equivalents

The indentified syntactic equivalents pairs include the sub-segments which sharing the same role in the same syntactic structure. Because of this, we can obtain a variation of a reference sentence by switching the two sub-segments of an equivalent pair in this sentence. This operation did not change the structure of the sentence but only replace a sub-segment in the structure with its equivalent.

Consequently, two new references can be generated by switching the two sub-segments of an equivalent pair between two reference sentences. Furthermore when we switch the sub-segments of all equivalent pairs between the two references, multiple new references are generated with various combinations of the switches. This operation is called the syntactic hybridization of the references which can be illustrated by following steps:

Suppose $R=\{r_i\}_{i=1...n}$ is a reference set containing n reference sentences to a single source sentence. R' is the new reference set containing the original reference sentences and the hybridized reference sentences. R' can be obtained by formula (1):

$$R' = \bigcup_{i=0}^{n} Equ(root_i) \quad (1)$$

where $root_i$ is the root node of the syntactic tree of r_i. *Equ(nt)* returns the set of all equivalent of the sub-segments covered by the tree node *nt*. The detailed process of *Equ(nt)* is:

Equ(nt):

Define set equ = Φ
Add Seg(nt) to equ
If nt is included in an equivalent pair <nt, nt', s, s'>
  Add p' to equ
  Define $child_{i=1...m}$ is the m children of nt
  Define hybr = $Equ(child_1) \times Equ(child_2) ... \times Equ(child_m)$
  Merge hybr into equ
Return equ

where *Seg(nt)* is the sub-segment covered by the tree node *nt*. Operation $S_1 \times S_2$ generates the Cartesian product of the sub-segment set S_1 and S_2, i.e. for each arbitrary sub-segment pair s_1 and s_2 selected from S_1 and S respectively, we concatenate s_1 and s_2. Finally, the reduplicate references in R' are removed.

For the example in Section 2, eight hybridized references can be generated including the original two sentences:

- Machine Translation develops constantly
- Machine Translation develops persistently
- Machine Translation progresses constantly
- Machine Translation progresses persistently
- MT develops constantly
- MT develops persistently
- MT progresses constantly
- MT progresses persistently

4 Experiments

We will show experimental results in this section to verify the effectiveness of the extended set of hybridized reference sentences. In the experiments, multiple translations of the source language sentences are evaluated with several popular automatic evaluation metrics. The evaluation is carried out on sentence level using the original reference set and the extended reference set respectively. Finally, the Pearson's correlations between the human assessments and evaluation scores using two reference set are calculated and compared.

The multiple translations and human assessments are obtained from the dataset of the MT evaluation workshop at ACL05 (LDC2006T04) and the dataset from NistMATR08 (LDC2008E43). Table 1 & 2 describes the detail of the two datasets.

The popular automatic evaluation metrics include BLEU (Papieni et al., 2002), GTM (Melamed et al., 2003), Rouge (Lin and Och, 2004) and METEOR (Banerjee and Lavie, 2005). The syntactic trees of the reference sentences are obtained with the Stanford statistical parser (Klein 2003) for LDC2006T04 and Collins parser (Collins 1999) for LDC2008E43.

Table 3 & 4 gives out the correlations using two reference set on both datasets. The first column is the name of the used metrics. The second column is the correlations based on the original reference set. The third column is the correlations based on the extended reference set. In the experiment, the maximum length of N-gram in BLEU is 4. The exponent of GTM is 2. ROUGE uses skip-bigram with a window of nine words. And METEOR is run in "exact" mode.

Release Year	2006
Genre	Newswire
Number of segments	919
Source Language	Chinese
Target Language	English
Number of system translations	7
Number of reference translations	4
Human assessment scores	Score 1-5, adequacy & fluency

Table 1 Description of LDC2006T04

Release Year	2008
Genre	Newswire
Number of segments	249
Source Language	Arabic
Target Language	English
Number of system translations	8
Number of reference translations	4
Human assessment scores	Score 1-7, adequacy

Table 2 Description of LDC2008E43

After the hybridization, each source sentence in LDC2006T04 has 31 corresponding reference sentences in average and each source sentence in LDC2008E43 has 66 corresponding reference sentences in average. The number of the references is greatly increased. And as shown in the results, the usage of the extended reference set improves the correlations with human assessments for all the metrics in most cases except the ROUGE on LDC 2008E43.

Metric	Original	Extended
BLEU	0.3488	0.3564
GTM	0.3671	0.3681
ROUGE	0.4252	0.4325
METEOR	0.4686	0.4723

Table 3 Pearson's correlations with human assessments on sentence level on LDC2006T04

Metric	Original	Extended
BLEU	0.6092	0.6109
GTM	0.5434	0.5438
ROUGE	**0.6628**	**0.6582**
METEOR	0.7053	0.7089

Table 4 Pearson's correlations with human assessments on sentence level on LDC2008E43

The following is a real instance in the experiments from LDC2008E43:

Four original references:

- Ten churches burned down in 10 days in the American state of Alabama
- Burning of ten churches in ten days in the American state of Alabama
- Ten churches set on fire in ten days in American state of Alabama
- Torching of ten churches within ten days in American state of Alabama

Six additional references:

- Torching of ten churches in ten days in the American state of Alabama
- Torching of ten churches within ten days in the American state of Alabama
- Torching of ten churches in ten days in American state of Alabama
- Burning of ten churches within ten days in American state of Alabama
- Burning of ten churches within ten days in the American state of Alabama
- Burning of ten churches in ten days in American state of Alabama

The syntactic structure of the original references:

- (TOP (S (NPB (CD Ten) (NNS Churches)) (VP (VBN Burned) (PP (IN Down) (PP (IN in) (NP (NPB (CD 10) (NNS Days)) (PP (IN in) (NP (NPB (DT the) (NNP American) (NNP State)) (PP (IN of) (NPB (NNP Alabama))))))))))
- (TOP (NP (NPB (NN Burning)) (PP (IN of) (NP (NPB (CD Ten) (NNS Churches)) (PP (IN in) (NP (NPB (CD Ten) (NNS Days)) (PP (IN in) (NP (NPB (DT the) (NNP American) (NNP State)) (PP (IN of) (NPB (NNP Alabama))))))))))
- (TOP (S (NPB (CD Ten) (NNS Churches)) (VP (VB Set) (PP (IN on) (NPB (NN Fire))) (PP (IN in) (NP (NPB (CD Ten) (NNS Days)) (PP (IN in) (NP (NPB (NNP American) (NNP State)) (PP (IN of) (NPB (NNP Alabama)))))))))
- (TOP (NP (NPB (NNP Torching)) (PP (IN of) (NP (NPB (CD Ten) (NNS Churches)) (PP (IN within) (NP (NPB (CD Ten) (NNS Days)) (PP (IN in) (NP (NPB (NNP American) (NNP State)) (PP (IN of) (NPB (NNP Alabama))))))))))

To investigate the distribution of the equivalents we also perform several statistics about the count and the length of the syntactic nodes. In table 5, we list the information about the count of the nodes. The first row is the average words count per reference sentence. The second and third row is the count of all tree nodes and equivalent nodes in all references respectively. The fourth and fifth row is the average count of tree nodes and equivalent nodes per reference sentence respectively.

	2006T04	2008E43
Average length of reference	31.52	34.43
Total tree nodes	211231	62569
Total equivalent nodes	21807	10073
Average tree nodes	57.46	62.82
Average equivalent nodes	5.93	10.11

Table 5 Counts of the tree nodes and equivalent nodes in references.

We also investigate the distribution of the length (count of covered words) of the nodes. First, we count the tree nodes and equivalent nodes whose length is from 1 word to 50 words. Then we calculate the pro-portion of equivalent nodes and tree nodes for each length. Figure 2 and 3 illustrate the distribution of absolute count of the equivalent nodes. The X-axis is the length of the nodes and the Y-axis is the count. Figure 4 and 5 illustrate the distribution of the proportions on two datasets respectively. The X-axis is the length of the nodes and the Y-axis is the proportion.

The investigation reveals four main messages. First, the absolute counts of the short equivalents are much more than those of long equivalents as expected. Second, the proportion of the long equivalents is greater than those of short equivalents, this clarify that the reason of large amount of short equivalents is the large amount of short tree nodes. Third, also from the proportion of view we can see that the new method comparably bias to the long equivalents. This happens because the method adopts a top-down survey of the tree. Forth, the multiple references in Arabic-English data seem to match each other better than the references in Chinese-English data. Arabic-English references have much more equivalents than Chinese-English data and bias to long equivalents more significant.

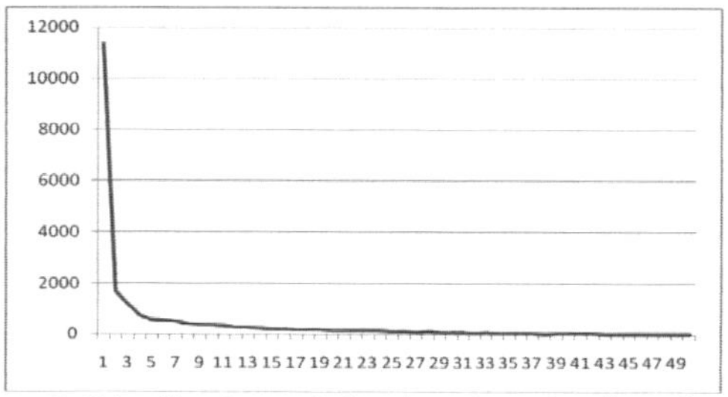

Figure 2 Distribution of absolute length of equivalent node on LDC2006T04

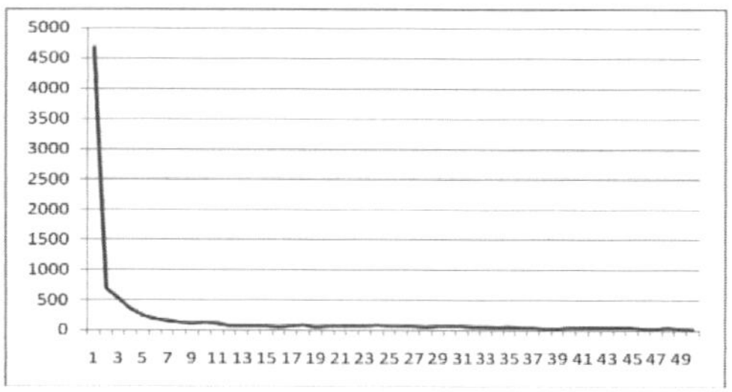

Figure 3 Distribution of absolute length of equivalent node on LDC2008E43

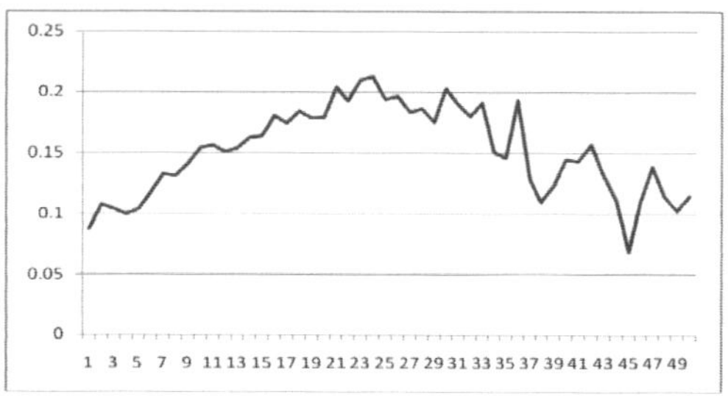

Figure 4 Distribution of length proportion of equivalent nodes on LDC2006T04

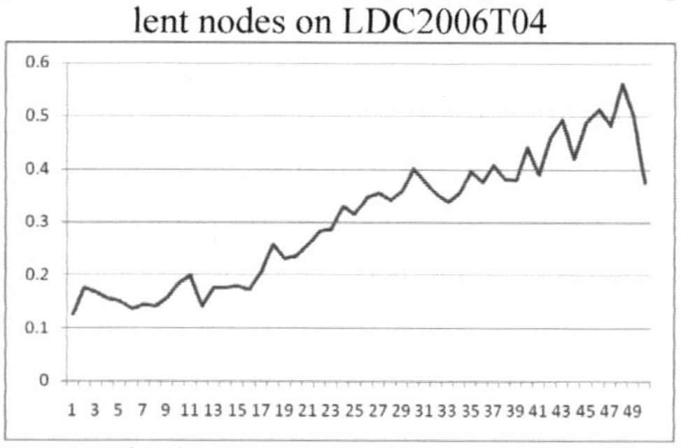

Figure 5 Distribution of length proportion of equivalent nodes on LDC2008E43

5 Discussion

The experimental results verify the positive effect of the hybridized reference for the automatic evaluation in most cases. Though the improvement of the correlations is not very significant it is stable across the metrics in various styles.

Compared with the previous works based on paraphrase and synonym the new method has three important advantages. The first is that the hybridized reference can switch the long span sub-segments beyond the words and phrases.

The second is that the switch can be per-formed in multiple levels, i.e. a sub-segment can not only be replaced as a single unit but also can be varied by replacing some child sub-segments of it. It's noticeable that the multiple level switches also make it possible to present some structural variations by means of the lexical variations. In hybridization, we can realize some structural variation between syntactic nodes by switch their parent node instead of reordering them directly.

The third advantage is that the new method needs no external knowledge which greatly facilitates the application. But this advantage also results in the main deficiency of this approach: the hybridization references cannot adopt any novel equivalents which are absent in existing references. This deficiency can be overcome by introducing the paraphrase and synonym into the syntactic hybridization.

It should be indicated that though the hybridization process generate many new references not all of the new references are reasonable.

In table 6 we compare the effect of hybridized references and manual references with more details on LDC2006T04. In the table, the first column is the contents of the references for each source sentence. "Manual" means the manual references and the number in front of it indicates how many manual references are provided. "Hybr" means the hybridized references generated from the manual references in front of the "+". The second column is the Pearson's correlations between human assessments and the BLEU scores using the corresponding reference set. Besides the set containing 4 references the other correlations are the average of the correlations based on all possible subset containing certain number of references. For example correlation of "2 Manual" is the average of the correlations based on 6 possible subset containing 2 references.

Reference Set	Correlation
1 Manual	0.2565

2 Manual	0.3057
2 Manual+ Hybr	0.3082
3 Manual	0.3316
3 Manual + Hybr	0.3369
4 Manual	0.3488
4 Manual+ Hybr	0.3564

Table 6 Pearson's correlations based on incremental reference set

As shown in the Table 6 hybridized references can improve the correlations with human assessments on different sizes of manual references set. But it also indicated that though hybridization can generate a mass of novel references the new references is always not more effective than even one additional manual references. This tells us that the quality of the hybridized references still need to be further refined.

Another message revealed by the table is that with the increase of the number of manual references the improvement of correlation made by additional manual references is decreasing. However, the improvement made by the hybridized is increasing. This happens because the number of hybridized references increases much faster than the number of manual references.

There are still several noticeable deficiencies of this work. First, it only works when there are more than two existing references. This make it cannot be used to extend the single reference in mass bilingual corpus. Second, which is also the most important one is that this method strongly focuses on the precision at the cost of recall. Though we have recognized many equivalents for each sentence but there are still many equivalents that share different context cannot be recognized. This will be our main future work. The last deficiency is the bias to the long equivalents. This problem is caused by the same reason with the second deficiency: this method define the equivalent with the same syntactic context. If two sub-nodes do not share the same parent it often have different brothers.

6 Conclusions and Future Work

In this work we present a novel method to extend the coverage of the reference set for the automatic evaluation of machine translation. The new method decomposes the existing references into sub-segments according to the syntactic structure. And then generate new reference sentences by hybridizing the equivalents of the segments which play the same syntactic role in corresponding references. In this way the new method can not only capture the equivalents of words and phrases like the other methods but also capture the equivalents of long sub-segments which are out of the capability of the other methods. Another important advantage of the new method is the no use of the external knowledge which greatly facilitates the application.

Experimental results show that with the extended reference set the state-of-the-arts automatic evaluation metrics achieve better correlation with the human assessments.

In the future work, we will relax the restriction of the equivalent definition and try to recognize more equivalents. We will also introduce the paraphrase and synonyms into our method to see further improvement. Another interesting challenge is to hybridize the equivalents in the different order and present the structural variations directly.

Acknowledgments

This work is supported by the National Natural Science Foundation of China under Grant No. 60773066 and 60736014, the National High Technology Development 863 Program of China under Grant No. 2006AA010108.

References

Statanjeev Banerjee, Alon Lavie. 2005. METEOR: An Automatic Metric for MT Evaluation with Im-proved Correlation with Human Judgements. In Proceedings of the ACL Workshop on Intrinsic and Extrinsic Evaluation Measures for Machine Trans-lation and/or Summarization.

M. Collins. 1999. Head-Driven Statistical Models for Natural Language Parsing. PhD Dissertation, University of Pennsylvania.

I. Dan Melamed, Ryan Green, Joseph P. Turian, 2003, Precision and recall of machine translation, In Proceedings of HLT/NAACL 2003.

David Kauchak, Regina Barzilay. 2006. Paraphrasing for Automatic Evaluation, In Proceedings of the NAACL 2006.

Dan Klein, Christopher Manning. 2003. Accurate Unlexicalized Parsing. In Proceedings of the 41th Meeting of the ACL, pp. 423-430.

Yves Lepage, Etienne Denoual. 2005. Automatic generation of paraphrases to be used as translation references in objective evaluation measures of ma-chine translation, In Proceedings of the IWP 2005.

Karolina Owczarzak, Declan Groves, Josef Van Genabith ,Andy Way. 2006. Contextual Bitext-Derived Paraphrases in Automatic MT Evaluation, In Proceedings of the Workshop on Statistical Ma-chine Translation.

Karolina Owczarzak, Josef Van Genabith, Andy Way. 2007. Dependency-Based Automatic Evaluation for Machine Translation, In Proceedings of SSST, NAACL-HLT 2007 / AMTA Workshop on Syntax and Structure in Statistical Translation.

Kishore Papieni, Salim Roukos, Todd Ward, Wei-Jing Zhu. 2002. BLEU: a method for automatic evaluation of machine translation, In Proceedings of the 40th Meeting of the ACL.

Grazia Russo-Lassner, Jimmy Lin, Philip Resnik. 2005. Re-evaluating Machine Translation Results with Paraphrase Support, Technical Report LAMP-TR-125/CS-TR-4754/UMIACS-TR-2005-57, University of Maryland, College Park, MD.

Chin-Yew Lin, Franz Josef Och. 2004. Automatic evaluation of machine translation quality using longest common subsequence and skip-bigram sta-tistics. In Proceedings of the 42th Meeting of the ACL.

Liang Zhou, Chin-Yew Lin, and Eduard Hovy. 2006. Re-evaluating Machine Translation Results with Paraphrase Support, In Proceedings of the EMNLP 2006.

A Study of Translation Rule Classification for Syntax-based Statistical Machine Translation

Hongfei Jiang, Sheng Li, Muyun Yang and Tiejun Zhao
School of Computer Science and Technology
Harbin Institute of Technology
{hfjiang,lisheng,ymy,tjzhao}@mtlab.hit.edu.cn

Abstract

Recently, numerous statistical machine translation models which can utilize various kinds of translation rules are proposed. In these models, not only the conventional syntactic rules but also the non-syntactic rules can be applied. Even the pure phrase rules are includes in some of these models. Although the better performances are reported over the conventional phrase model and syntax model, the mixture of diversified rules still leaves much room for study. In this paper, we present a refined rule classification system. Based on this classification system, the rules are classified according to different standards, such as lexicalization level and generalization. Especially, we refresh the concepts of the structure reordering rules and the discontiguous phrase rules. This novel classification system may supports the SMT research community with some helpful references.

1 Introduction

Phrase-based statistical machine translation models (Marcu and Wong, 2002; Koehn et al., 2003; Och and Ney, 2004; Koehn, 2004; Koehn et al., 2007) have achieved significant improvements in translation accuracy over the original IBM word-based model. However, there are still many limitations in phrase based models. The most frequently pointed limitation is its inefficacy to modeling the structure reordering and the discontiguous corresponding. To overcome these limitations, many syntax-based SMT models have been proposed (Wu, 1997; Chiang, 2007; Ding et al., 2005; Eisner, 2003; Quirk et al., 2005; Liu et al., 2007; Zhang et al., 2007; Zhang et al., 2008a; Zhang et al., 2008b; Gildea, 2003; Galley et al., 2004; Marcu et al., 2006; Bod, 2007). The basic motivation behind syntax-based model is that the syntax information has the potential to model the structure reordering and discontiguous corresponding by the intrinsic structural generalization ability. Although remarkable progresses have been reported, the strict syntactic constraint (the both sides of the rules should strictly be a subtree of the whole syntax parse) greatly hinders the utilization of the non-syntactic translation equivalents. To alleviate this constraint, a few works have attempted to make full use of the non-syntactic rules by extending their syntax-based models to more general frameworks. For example, forest-to-string transformation rules have been integrated into the tree-to-string translation framework by (Liu et al., 2006; Liu et al., 2007). Zhang et al. (2008a) made it possible to utilize the non-syntactic rules and even the phrases which are used in phrase based model by advancing a general tree sequence to tree sequence framework based on the tree-to-tree model presented in (Zhang et al., 2007). In these models, various kinds of rules can be employed. For example, as shown in Figure 1 and Figure 2, Figure 1 shows a Chinese-to-English sentence pair with syntax parses on both sides and the word alignments (dotted lines). Figure 2 lists some of the rules which can be extracted from the sentence pair in Figure 1 by the system used in (Zhang et al., 2008a). These rules includes not only conventional syntax rules but also the tree sequence rules (the multi-headed syntax rules). Even the phrase rules are adopted by

Proceedings of SSST-3, Third Workshop on Syntax and Structure in Statistical Translation, pages 45–50,
Boulder, Colorado, June 2009.

the system. Although the better performances are reported over the conventional phrase-based model and syntax-based model, the mixture of diversified rules still leaves much room for study. Given such a hybrid rule set, we must want to know what kinds of rules can make more important contributions to the overall system performance and what kinds of rules are redundant compared with the others. From engineering point of view, the developers may concern about which kinds of rules should be preferred and which kinds of rules could be discard without too much decline in translation quality. However, one of the precondition for the investigations of these issues is what are the "rule categories"? In other words, some comprehensive rule classifications are necessary to make the rule analyses feasible. The motivation of this paper is to present such a rule classification.

2 Related Works

A few researches have made some exploratory investigations towards the effects of different rules by classifying the translation rules into different subcategories (Liu et al., 2007; Zhang et al., 2008a; DeNeefe et al., 2007). Liu et al. (2007) differentiated the rules in their tree-to-string model which integrated with forest[1]-to-string into fully lexicalized rules, non-lexicalized rules and partial lexicalized rules according to the lexicalization levels. As an extension, Zhang et al. (2008a) proposed two more categories: Structure Reordering Rules (SRR) and Discontiguous Phrase Rules (DPR). The SRR stands for the rules which have at least two non-terminal leaf nodes with inverted order in the source and target side. And DPR refers to the rules having at least one non-terminal leaf node between two terminal leaf nodes. (DeNeefe et al., 2007) made an illuminating breakdown of the different kinds of rules. Firstly, they classify all the GHKM[2] rules (Galley et al., 2004; Galley et al., 2006) into two categories: lexical rules and non-lexical rules. The former are the rules whose source side has no source words. In other words, a non-lexical rule is a purely abstract rule. The latter is the complementary set of the former. And then lexical rules are classified further into phrasal rules and non-phrasal rules. The *phrasal rules* refer to the rules whose source side and the yield of the target side contain exactly one contiguous phrase each. And the one or more nonterminals can be placed on either side of the phrase. In other words, each phrasal rule can be simulated by the conjunction of two more phrase rules. (DeNeefe et al., 2007) classifies non-phrasal rules further into structural rules, re-ordering rules, and noncontiguous phrase rules. However, these categories are not explicitly defined in (DeNeefe et al., 2007) since out of its focus. Our proposed rule classification is inspired by these works.

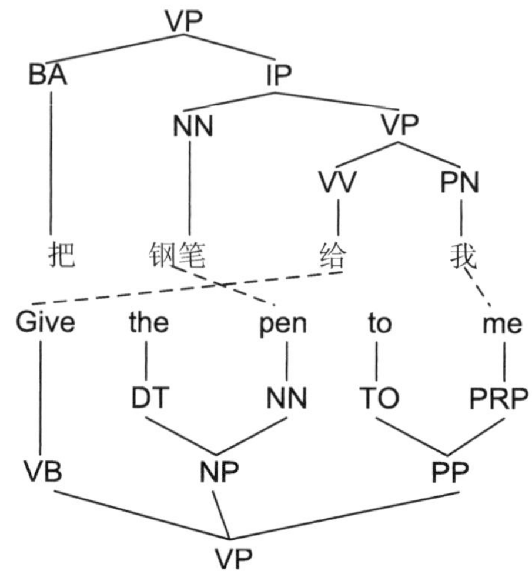

Figure 1: A syntax tree pair example. Dotted lines stands for the word alignments.

3 Rules Classifications

Currently, there have been several classifications in SMT research community. Generally, the rules can be classified into two main groups according to whether syntax information is involved: bilingual phrases (Phrase) and syntax rules (Syntax). Further, the syntax rules can be divided into three categories according to the lexicalization levels (Liu et al., 2007; Zhang et al., 2008a):

1) Fully lexicalized (FLex): all leaf nodes in both the source and target sides are lexicons (terminals)

2) Unlexicalized (ULex): all leaf nodes in both the

[1] A "forest" means a sub-tree sequence derived from a given parse tree

[2] One reviewer asked about the acronym **GHKM**. We guess it is an acronym for the authors of (Galley et al., 2004): Michel **G**alley, Mark **H**opkins, Kevin **K**night and Daniel **M**arcu.

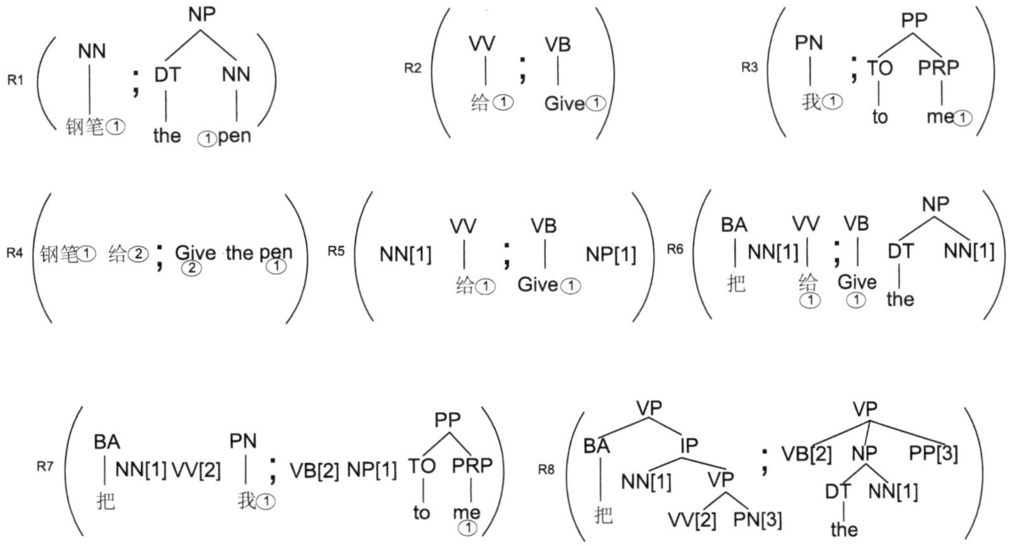

Figure 2: Some rules can be extracted by the system used in (Zhang et al., 2008a) from the sentence pair in Figure 1.

source and target sides are non-lexicons (non-terminals)

3) Partially lexicalized (PLex): otherwise.

In Figure 2, R_1-R_3 are FLex rules, and R_5-R_8 are PLex rules.

Following (Zhang et al., 2008b), a syntax rule r can be formalized into a tuple

$$< \xi_s, \xi_t, A_T, A_{NT} >$$

, where ξ_s and ξ_t are tree sequences of source side and target side respectively, A_T is a many-to-many correspondence set which includes the alignments between the terminal leaf nodes from source and target side, and A_{NT} is a one-to-one correspondence set which includes the synchronizing relations between the non-terminal leaf nodes from source and target side.

Then, the syntax rules can also fall into two categories according to whether equipping with generalization capability (Chiang, 2007; Zhang et al., 2008a):

1) Initial rules (Initial): all leaf nodes of this rule are terminals.

2) Abstract rules (Abstract): otherwise, i.e. at least one leaf node is a non-terminal.

A non-terminal leaf node in a rule is named an **abstract node** since it has the generalization capability. Comparing these two classifications for syntax rules, we can find that a FLex rule is a initial rule when ULex rules and PLex rules belong to abstract rules.

These classifications are clear and easy for understanding. However, we argue that they need further refinement for in-depth study. Specially, more refined differentiations are needed for the abstract rules (ULex rules and PLex rules) since they play important roles for the characteristic capabilities which are deemed to be the advantages over the phrase-based model. For instance, the potentials to model the structure reordering and the discontiguous correspondence. The Structure Reordering Rules (SRR) and Discontiguous Phrase Rules (DPR) mentioned by (Zhang et al., 2008a) can be regarded as more in-depth classification of the syntax rules. In (Zhang et al., 2008a), they are described as follows:

Definition 1: The **Structure Reordering Rule (SRR)** refers to the structure reordering rule that has at least two non-terminal leaf nodes with inverted order in the source and target side.

Definition 2: The **Discontiguous Phrase Rule (DPR)** refers to the rule having at least one non-terminal leaf node between two lexicalized leaf nodes.

Based on these descriptions, R_7, R_8 in Figure 2 belong to the category of SRR and R_6, R_7 fall into the category of DPR. Although these two definitions are easy implemented in practice, we argue that the definition of SRR is not complete. The reordering rules involving the reordering between content word terminals and non-terminal (such as R_5 in Figure 2) also can model the useful structure reorderings. Moreover, it is not uncommon that a rule demonstrates the reorderings between two non-terminals as well as the reorderings between one non-terminal and one content word terminal. The reason for our emphasis of content word terminal is that the reorderings between the non-terminals and function word are less meaningful.

One of the theoretical problems with phrase based SMT models is that they can not effectively model the discontiguous translations and numerous attempts have been made on this issue (Simard et al., 2005; Quirk and Menezes, 2006; Wellington et al., 2006; Bod, 2007; Zhang et al., 2007). What seems to be lacking, however, is a explicit definition to the discontiguous translation. The definition of DPR in (Zhang et al., 2008a) is explicit but somewhat rough and not very accurate. For example, in Figure 3(a), non-terminal node pair ([0,'爱'], [0,'love']) is surrounded by lexical terminals. According to Definition 2, it is a DPR. However, obviously it is not a discontiguous phrase actually. This rule can be simulated by conjunctions of three phrases ('我', 'I'; '爱', 'love'; '你','you'). In contrast, the translation rule in Figure 3(b) is an actual discontiguous phrase rule. The English correspondences of the Chinese word '关' is dispersed in the English side in which the correspondence of Chinese word '灯' is inserted. This rule can not be simulated by any conjunctions of the sub phrases. It must be noted that the discontiguous phrase ('关'-"switch ... off") can not be abstracted under the existing synchronous grammar frameworks. The fundamental reason is that the corresponding parts should be abstracted in the same time and lexicalized in the same time. In other words, the discontiguous phrase can not be modeled by the permutation between non-terminals (abstract nodes). Another point to notice is that our focus in this paper is the ability demonstrated by the abstract rules. Thus, we do not pay much attentions to the reorderings and discontiguous phrases involved in the phrase rules (e.g. "关 灯"-"switch the light off") since they lack the generalization capability. Therefore, the discontiguous phrase is limited to the relation between non-terminals and terminals.

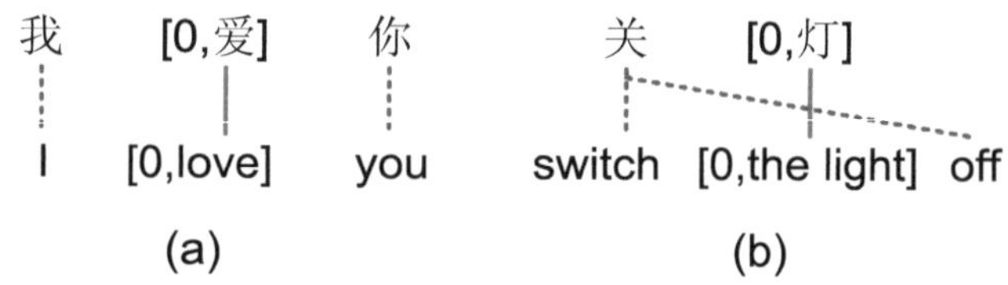

Figure 3: Examples for demonstrating the actual discontiguous phrase. (a) is a negative example for the definition of DPR in (Zhang et al., 2008a), (b) is a actual discontiguous phrase rule.

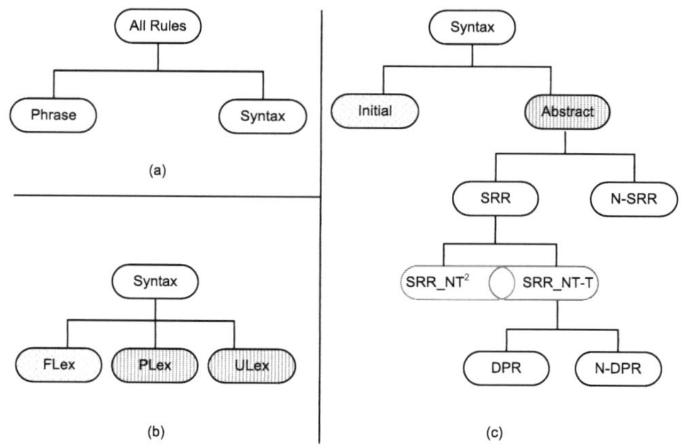

Figure 4: The rule classifications used in this paper. (a) shows that the rules can be divided into phrase rules and syntax rules according to whether a rule includes the syntactic information. (b) illustrates that the syntax rules can be classified into three kinds according to the lexicalization level. (c) shows that the abstract rules can be classified into more refined sub-categories.

On the basis of the above analyses, we present a novel classification system for the abstract rules based on the crossings between the leaf node alignment links. Given an abstract rule $r = <\xi_s, \xi_t, A_T, A_{NT}>$, it is

1) a Structure Reordering Rule (SRR), if $\exists$ a link $l \in A_{NT}$ is crossed with a link $l' \in \{A_T \cap A_{NT}\}$
   a) a SRR_NT^2 rule, if the link $l' \in A_{NT}$
   b) a SRR_NT-T rule, if the link $l' \in A_T$
2) not a Structure Reordering Rule (N-SRR), otherwise.

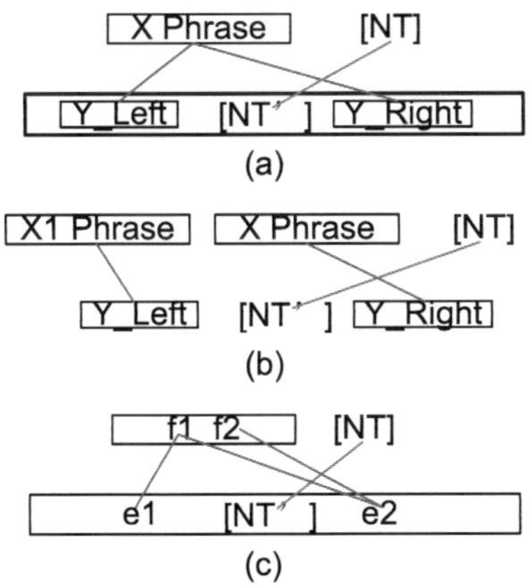

Figure 5: The patterns to show the characteristics of discontiguous phrase rules.

Note that the intersection of SRR_NT^2 and SRR_NT-T is not necessary an empty set, i.e. a rule can be both SRR_NT^2 and SRR_NT-T rule.

The basic characteristic of the discontiguous translation is that the correspondence of one non-terminal NT is inserted among the correspondences of one phrase X. Figure 5 (a) illustrates this situation. However, this characteristic can not support necessary and sufficient condition. For example, if the phrase X can be divided like Figure 5 (b), then the rule in Figure 5 (a) is actually a reordering rule rather than a discontiguous phrase rule. For sufficient condition, we constrain that the phrase $X = w_i \ldots w_j$ need to satisfy the requirement: w_i should be connected with w_j through word alignment links (A word is connected with itself). In Figure 5(c), f_1 is connected with f_2 when NT' is inserted between e_1 and e_2. Thus, the rule in Figure 5(c) is a discontiguous phrase rule.

Definition 3: Given an abstract rule $r =< \xi_s, \xi_t, A_T, A_{NT} >$, it is a **Discontiguous Phrase** iff $\exists$ two links l_{t1}, l_{t2} from A_T and a link l_{nt} from A_{NT}, satisfy: l_{t1}, l_{t2} are emitted from the same word and l_{t1} is crossed with l_{nt} when l_{t2} is not crossed with l_{nt}.

Through Definition 3, we know that the DPR is a sub-set of the SRR_NT-T.

4 Conclusions and Future Works

In this paper, we present a refined rule classification system. Based on this classification system, the rules are classified according to different standards, such as lexicalization level and generalization. Especially, we refresh the concepts of the structure reordering rules and the discontiguous phrase rules. This novel classification system may supports the SMT research community with some helpful references.

In the future works, aiming to analyze the rule contributions and the redundances issues using the presented rule classification based on some real translation systems, we plan to implement some synchronous grammar based syntax translation models such as the one presented in (Liu et al., 2007) or in (Zhang et al., 2008a). Taking such a system as the experimental platform, we can perform comprehensive statistics about distributions of different rule categories. What is more important, the contribution of each rule category can be evaluated seriatim. Furthermore, which kinds of rules are preferentially applied in the 1-best decoding can be studied. All these investigations could reveal very useful information for the optimization of rule extraction and the improvement of the computational models for synchronous grammar based machine translation.

Acknowledgments

This work is supported by the Key Program of National Natural Science Foundation of China (60736014), and the Key Project of the National High Technology Research and Development Program of China (2006AA010108).

References

Rens Bod. 2007. Unsupervised syntax-based machine translation: The contribution of discontiguous phrases. In *Proceedings of Machine Translation Summit XI 2007*,Copenhagen, Denmark.

David Chiang. 2007. Hierarchical phrase-based translation. In *computational linguistics*, 33(2).

Ding, Y. and Palmer, M. 2005. Machine translation using probabilistic synchronous dependency insertion grammars In *Proceedings of ACL.*

DeNeefe, S. and Knight, K. and Wang, W. and Marcu, D. 2007. What can syntax-based MT learn from phrase-based MT? In *Proceedings of EMNLP/CONLL.*

Michel Galley, Mark Hopkins, Kevin Knight and Daniel Marcu. 2004. What's in a translation rule? In *Proceedings of NAACL-HLT 2004*, pages 273-280.

Galley, M. and Graehl, J. and Knight, K. and Marcu, D. and DeNeefe, S. and Wang, W. and Thayer, I. 2006. Scalable inference and training of context-rich syntactic translation models In *Proceedings of ACL-COLING*

Daniel Gildea 2003. Loosely Tree-Based Alignment for Machine Translation. In *Proceedings of ACL 2003*, pages 80-87.

Jason Eisner. 2003. Learning non-isomorphic tree mappings for machine translation. In *Proceedings of ACL 2003*.

Philipp Koehn, Franz Joseph Och, and Daniel Marcu. 2003. Statistical phrase-based translation. In *Proceedings of HLT/NAACL 2003*, pages 127-133, Edmonton, Canada, May.

Philipp Koehn. 2004. Pharaoh: a beam search decoder for phrase-based statistical machine translation models. In *Proceedings of the Sixth Conference of the Association for Machine Translation in the Americas*, pages 115-124.

Philipp Koehn, Hieu Hoang, Alexandra Birch, Chris Callison-Burch, Marcello Federico, Nicola Bertoldi, Brooke Cowan, Wade Shen, Christine Moran, Richard Zens, Chris Dyer, Ondrej Bojar, Alexandra Constantin, Evan Herbst. 2007. Moses: open source toolkit for statistical machine translation. ACL 2007, demonstration session, Prague, Czech Republic, June 2007.

Yang Liu, Qun Liu, Shouxun Lin. 2006. Tree-to-string alignment template for statistical machine translation. In *Proceedings of ACL-COLING*.

Yang Liu, Yun Huang, Qun Liu, and Shouxun Lin. 2007. Forest-to-string statistical translation rules. In *Proceedings of ACL 2007*, pages 704-711.

Daniel Marcu and William Wong. 2002. A phrase based, joint probability model for statistical machine translation. In *Proceedings of EMNLP*.

Daniel Marcu, Wei Wang, Abdessamad Echihabi, and Kevin Knight. 2006. SPMT: Statistical machine translation with syntactified target language Phrases. In *Proceedings of EMNLP*.

Franz Josef Och and Hermann Ney. 2000. Improved statistical alignment models. In *Proceedings of ACL 2000*, pages 440-447.

Franz Josef Och and Herman Ney. 2004. The alignment template approach to statistical machine translation. *Computational Linguistics*, 30(4):417-449.

Chris Quirk, Arul Menezes, and Colin Cherry. 2005. Dependency treelet translation: Syntactically informed phrasal SMT. In *Proceedings of ACL 2005*, pages 271-279, Ann Arbor, Michigan, June.

Chris Quirk and Arul Menezes. 2006. Do we need phrases? Challenging the conventional wisdom in Statistical Machine Translation. In *Proceedings of HLT/NAACL*

Simard, M. and Cancedda, N. and Cavestro, B. and Dymetman, M. and Gaussier, E. and Goutte, C. and Yamada, K. and Langlais, P. and Mauser, A. 2005. Translating with non-contiguous phrases. In *Proceedings of HLT-EMNLP*, volume 2, pages 901-904.

Benjamin Wellington, Sonjia Waxmonsky and I. Dan Melamed. 2006. Empirical Lower Bounds on the Complexity of Translational Equivalence. In *Proceedings of ACL-COLING 2006*, pages 977-984.

Dekai Wu. 1997. Stochastic inversion transduction grammars and bilingual parsing of parallel corpora. In *Proceedings of ACL 1997. Computational Linguistics*, 23(3):377-403.

Min Zhang, Hongfei Jiang, Ai Ti AW, Jun Sun, Sheng Li, and Chew Lim Tan. 2007. A tree-to-tree alignment-based model for statistical machine translation. In *Proceedings of Machine Translation Summit XI 2007*,Copenhagen, Denmark.

Min Zhang, Hongfei Jiang, Ai Ti AW, Haizhou Li, Chew Lim Tan and Sheng Li. 2008a. A tree sequence alignment-based tree-to-tree translation model. In *Proceedings of ACL-HLT*

Min Zhang, Hongfei Jiang, Haizhou Li, Ai Ti AW, and Sheng Li. 2008b. Grammar Comparison Study for Translational Equivalence Modeling and Statistical Machine Translation. In *Proceedings of Coling*

Discriminative Reordering with Chinese Grammatical Relations Features

Pi-Chuan Chang[a], **Huihsin Tseng**[b], **Dan Jurafsky**[a], and **Christopher D. Manning**[a]
[a]Computer Science Department, Stanford University, Stanford, CA 94305
[b]Yahoo! Inc., Santa Clara, CA 95054
{pichuan,jurafsky,manning}@stanford.edu, huihui@yahoo-inc.com

Abstract

The prevalence in Chinese of grammatical structures that translate into English in different word orders is an important cause of translation difficulty. While previous work has used phrase-structure parses to deal with such ordering problems, we introduce a richer set of Chinese grammatical relations that describes more semantically abstract relations between words. Using these Chinese grammatical relations, we improve a phrase orientation classifier (introduced by Zens and Ney (2006)) that decides the ordering of two phrases when translated into English by adding path features designed over the Chinese typed dependencies. We then apply the log probability of the phrase orientation classifier as an extra feature in a phrase-based MT system, and get significant BLEU point gains on three test sets: MT02 (+0.59), MT03 (+1.00) and MT05 (+0.77). Our Chinese grammatical relations are also likely to be useful for other NLP tasks.

1 Introduction

Structural differences between Chinese and English are a major factor in the difficulty of machine translation from Chinese to English. The wide variety of such Chinese-English differences include the ordering of head nouns and relative clauses, and the ordering of prepositional phrases and the heads they modify. Previous studies have shown that using syntactic structures from the source side can help MT performance on these constructions. Most of the previous syntactic MT work has used phrase structure parses in various ways, either by doing syntax-directed translation to directly translate parse trees into strings in the target language (Huang et al., 2006), or by using source-side parses to preprocess the source sentences (Wang et al., 2007).

One intuition for using syntax is to capture different Chinese structures that might have the same

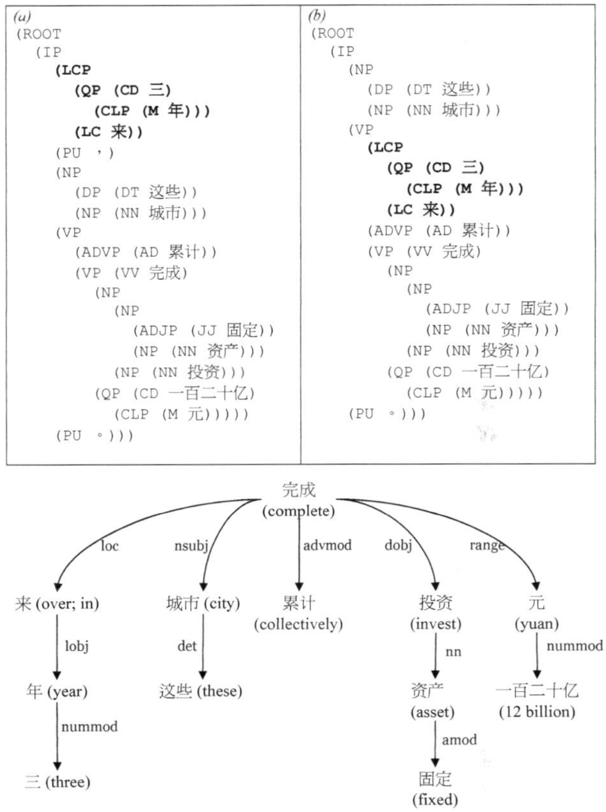

Figure 1: Sentences (*a*) and (*b*) have the same meaning, but different phrase structure parses. Both sentences, however, have the same typed dependencies shown at the bottom of the figure.

meaning and hence the same translation in English. But it turns out that phrase structure (and linear order) are not sufficient to capture this meaning relation. Two sentences with the same meaning can have different phrase structures and linear orders. In the example in Figure 1, sentences (*a*) and (*b*) have the same meaning, but different *linear orders* and different *phrase structure parses*. The translation of sentence (*a*) is: "*In the past three years* these municipalities have collectively put together investment in fixed assets in the amount of 12 billion yuan." In sentence (*b*), "in the past three years" has moved its

Proceedings of SSST-3, Third Workshop on Syntax and Structure in Statistical Translation, pages 51–59,
Boulder, Colorado, June 2009.

position. The temporal adverbial "三年来" (in the past three years) has different linear positions in the sentences. The phrase structures are different too: in (*a*) the `LCP` is immediately under `IP` while in (*b*) it is under `VP`.

We propose to use *typed dependency* parses instead of phrase structure parses. Typed dependency parses give information about grammatical relations between words, instead of constituency information. They capture syntactic relations, such as *nsubj* (nominal subject) and *dobj* (direct object) , but also encode semantic information such as in the *loc* (localizer) relation. For the example in Figure 1, if we look at the sentence structure from the typed dependency parse (bottom of Figure 1), "三年来" is connected to the main verb 完成 (finish) by a *loc* (localizer) relation, and the structure is the same for sentences (*a*) and (*b*). This suggests that this kind of semantic and syntactic representation could have more benefit than phrase structure parses.

Our Chinese typed dependencies are automatically extracted from phrase structure parses. In English, this kind of typed dependencies has been introduced by de Marneffe and Manning (2008) and de Marneffe et al. (2006). Using typed dependencies, it is easier to read out relations between words, and thus the typed dependencies have been used in meaning extraction tasks.

We design features over the Chinese typed dependencies and use them in a phrase-based MT system when deciding whether one chunk of Chinese words (MT system statistical phrase) should appear before or after another. To achieve this, we train a discriminative phrase orientation classifier following the work by Zens and Ney (2006), and we use the grammatical relations between words as extra features to build the classifier. We then apply the phrase orientation classifier as a feature in a phrase-based MT system to help reordering.

2 Discriminative Reordering Model

Basic reordering models in phrase-based systems use linear distance as the cost for phrase movements (Koehn et al., 2003). The disadvantage of these models is their insensitivity to the content of the words or phrases. More recent work (Tillman, 2004; Och et al., 2004; Koehn et al., 2007) has introduced lexicalized reordering models which estimate reordering probabilities conditioned on the actual phrases. Lexicalized reordering models have brought significant gains over the baseline reordering models, but one concern is that data sparseness can make estimation less reliable. Zens and Ney (2006) proposed a discriminatively trained phrase orientation model and evaluated its performance as a classifier and when plugged into a phrase-based MT system. Their framework allows us to easily add in extra features. Therefore we use it as a testbed to see if we can effectively use features from Chinese typed dependency structures to help reordering in MT.

2.1 Phrase Orientation Classifier

We build up the target language (English) translation from left to right. The phrase orientation classifier predicts the start position of the next phrase in the source sentence. In our work, we use the simplest class definition where we group the start positions into two classes: one class for a position to the left of the previous phrase (*reversed*) and one for a position to the right (*ordered*).

Let $c_{j,j'}$ be the class denoting the movement from source position j to source position j' of the next phrase. The definition is:

$$c_{j,j'} = \begin{cases} \textit{reversed} & \text{if } j' < j \\ \textit{ordered} & \text{if } j' > j \end{cases}$$

The phrase orientation classifier model is in the log-linear form:

$$p_{\lambda_1^N}(c_{j,j'} | f_1^J, e_1^I, i, j) = \frac{\exp\left(\sum_{n=1}^{N} \lambda_n h_n(f_1^J, e_1^I, i, j, c_{j,j'})\right)}{\sum_{c'} \exp\left(\sum_{n=1}^{N} \lambda_n h_n(f_1^J, e_1^I, i, j, c')\right)}$$

i is the target position of the current phrase, and f_1^J and e_1^I denote the source and target sentences respectively. c' represents possible categories of $c_{j,j'}$.

We can train this log-linear model on lots of labeled examples extracted from all of the aligned MT training data. Figure 2 is an example of an aligned sentence pair and the labeled examples that can be extracted from it. Also, different from conventional MERT training, we can have a large number of binary features for the discriminative phrase orientation classifier. The experimental setting will be described in Section 4.1.

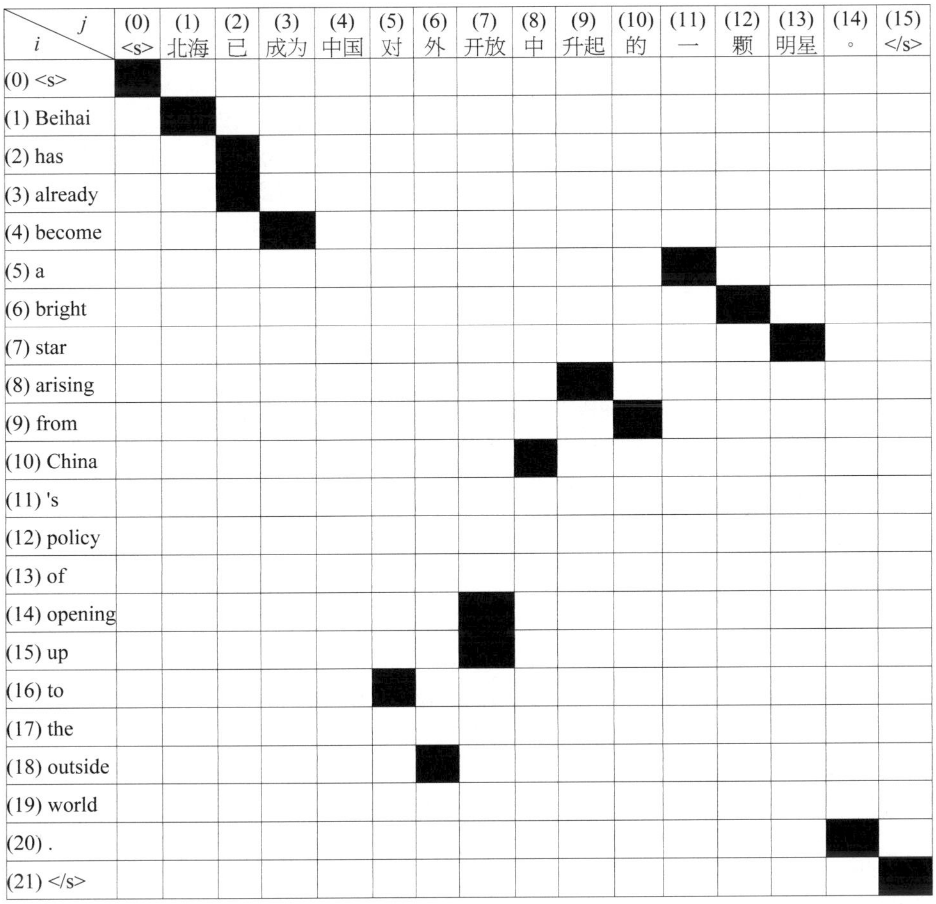

i	j	j'	class
0	0	1	ordered
1	1	2	ordered
3	2	3	ordered
4	3	11	ordered
5	11	12	ordered
6	12	13	ordered
7	**13**	**9**	**reversed**
8	9	10	ordered
9	**10**	**8**	**reversed**
10	**8**	**7**	**reversed**
15	**7**	**5**	**reversed**
16	5	6	ordered
18	6	14	ordered
20	14	15	ordered

Figure 2: An illustration of an alignment grid between a Chinese sentence and its English translation along with the labeled examples for the phrase orientation classifier. Note that the alignment grid in this example is automatically generated.

The basic feature functions are similar to what Zens and Ney (2006) used in their MT experiments. The basic binary features are source words within a window of size 3 ($d \in -1, 0, 1$) around the current source position j, and target words within a window of size 3 around the current target position i. In the classifier experiments in Zens and Ney (2006) they also use word classes to introduce generalization capabilities. In the MT setting it's harder to incorporate the part-of-speech information on the target language. Zens and Ney (2006) also exclude word class information in the MT experiments. In our work we will simply use the word features as basic features for the classification experiments as well. As a concrete example, we look at the labeled example $(i = 4, j = 3, j' = 11)$ in Figure 2. We include the word features in a window of size 3 around j and i as in Zens and Ney (2006), we also include words around j' as features. So we will have nine word features for $(i = 4, j = 3, j' = 11)$:

Src_{-1}:已	Src_0:成为	Src_1:中国
$Src2_{-1}$:的	$Src2_0$:一	$Src2_1$:颗
Tgt_{-1}:already	Tgt_0:become	Tgt_1:a

2.2 Path Features Using Typed Dependencies

Assuming we have parsed the Chinese sentence that we want to translate and have extracted the grammatical relations in the sentence, we design features using the grammatical relations. We use the path between the two words annotated by the grammatical relations. Using this feature helps the model learn about what the relation is between the two chunks of Chinese words. The feature is defined as follows: for two words at positions p and q in the Chinese

Shared relations	Chinese	English
nn	15.48%	6.81%
punct	12.71%	9.64%
nsubj	6.87%	4.46%
rcmod	2.74%	0.44%
dobj	6.09%	3.89%
advmod	4.93%	2.73%
conj	6.34%	4.50%
num/nummod	3.36%	1.65%
attr	0.62%	0.01%
tmod	0.79%	0.25%
ccomp	1.30%	0.84%
xsubj	0.22%	0.34%
cop	0.07%	0.85%
cc	2.06%	3.73%
amod	3.14%	7.83%
prep	3.66%	10.73%
det	1.30%	8.57%
pobj	2.82%	10.49%

Table 1: The percentage of typed dependencies in files 1–325 in Chinese (CTB6) and English (English-Chinese Translation Treebank)

sentence ($p < q$), we find the shortest path in the typed dependency parse from p to q, concatenate all the relations on the path and use that as a feature.

A concrete example is the sentences in Figure 3, where the alignment grid and labeled examples are shown in Figure 2. The glosses of the Chinese words in the sentence are in Figure 3, and the English translation is "Beihai has already become a bright star arising from China's policy of opening up to the outside world." which is also listed in Figure 2.

For the labeled example ($i = 4, j = 3, j' = 11$), we look at the typed dependency parse to find the path feature between 成为 and 一. The relevant dependencies are: *dobj*(成为, 明星), *clf*(明星, 颗) and *nummod*(颗, 一). Therefore the path feature is *PATH:dobjR-clfR-nummodR*. We also use the directionality: we add an *R* to the dependency name if it's going against the direction of the arrow.

3 Chinese Grammatical Relations

Our Chinese grammatical relations are designed to be very similar to the Stanford English typed dependencies (de Marneffe and Manning, 2008; de Marneffe et al., 2006).

3.1 Description

There are 45 named grammatical relations, and a default 46th relation *dep* (dependent). If a dependency matches no patterns, it will have the most generic relation *dep*. The descriptions of the 45 grammatical relations are listed in Table 2 ordered by their frequencies in files 1–325 of CTB6 (LDC2007T36). The total number of dependencies is 85748, and other than the ones that fall into the 45 grammatical relations, there are also 7470 dependencies (8.71% of all dependencies) that do not match any patterns, and therefore keep the generic name *dep*.

3.2 Chinese Specific Structures

Although we designed the typed dependencies to show structures that exist both in Chinese and English, there are many other syntactic structures that only exist in Chinese. The typed dependencies we designed also cover those Chinese specific structures. For example, the usage of "的" (DE) is one thing that could lead to different English translations. In the Chinese typed dependencies, there are relations such as *cpm* (DE as complementizer) or *assm* (DE as associative marker) that are used to mark these different structures. The Chinese-specific "把" (BA) construction also has a relation *ba* dedicated to it.

The typed dependencies annotate these Chinese specific relations, but do not directly provide a mapping onto how they are translated into English. It becomes more obvious how those structures affect the ordering when Chinese sentences are translated into English when we apply the typed dependencies as features in the phrase orientation classifier. This will be further discussed in Section 4.4.

3.3 Comparison with English

To compare the distribution of Chinese typed dependencies with English, we extracted the English typed dependencies from the translation of files 1–325 in the English Chinese Translation Treebank 1.0 (LDC2007T02), which correspond to files 1–325 in CTB6. The English typed dependencies are extracted using the Stanford Parser.

There are 116,799 total English dependencies, and 85,748 Chinese ones. On the corpus we use, there are 45 distinct dependency types (not including *dep*) in Chinese, and 50 in English. The coverage of named relations is 91.29% in Chinese and 90.48% in English; the remainder are the unnamed relation *dep*. We looked at the 18 shared relations

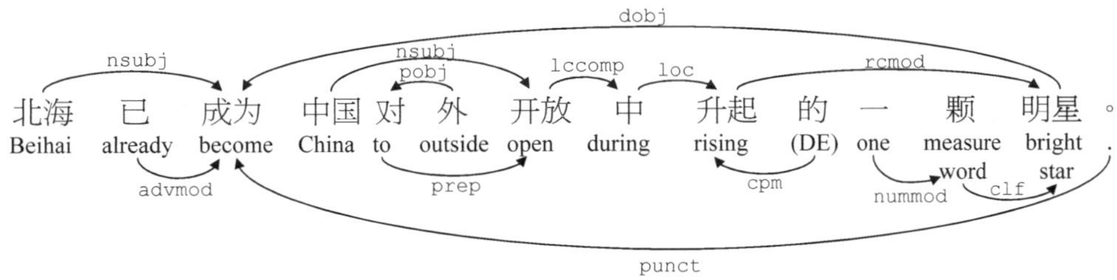

Figure 3: A Chinese example sentence labeled with typed dependencies

between Chinese and English in Table 1. Chinese has more *nn*, *punct*, *nsubj*, *rcmod*, *dobj*, *advmod*, *conj*, *nummod*, *attr*, *tmod*, and *ccomp* while English uses more *pobj*, *det*, *prep*, *amod*, *cc*, *cop*, and *xsubj*, due mainly to grammatical differences between Chinese and English. For example, some determiners in English (e.g., "the" in (1b)) are not mandatory in Chinese:

(1a) 进出口/import and export 总额/total value
(1b) The total value of imports and exports

In another difference, English uses adjectives (*amod*) to modify a noun ("financial" in (2b)) where Chinese can use noun compounds ("金融/finance" in (2a)).

(2a) 西藏/Tibet 金融/finance 体制/system 改革/reform
(2b) the reform in Tibet 's financial system

We also noticed some larger differences between the English and Chinese typed dependency distributions. We looked at specific examples and provide the following explanations.

prep* and *pobj English has much more uses of *prep* and *pobj*. We examined the data and found three major reasons:

1. Chinese uses both prepositions and postpositions while English only has prepositions. "After" is used as a postposition in Chinese example (3a), but a preposition in English (3b):
   (3a) 九七/1997 之後/after
   (3b) after 1997
2. Chinese uses noun phrases in some cases where English uses prepositions. For example, "之间" (period, or during) is used as a noun phrase in (4a), but it's a preposition in English.
   (4a) 九七/1997 到/to 九八/1998 之间 /period
   (4b) during 1997-1998
3. Chinese can use noun phrase modification in situations where English uses prepositions. In example (5a), Chinese does not use any prepositions between "apple company" and "new product", but English requires use of either "of" or "from".
   (5a) 苹果公司/apple company 新产品/new product
   (5b) the new product of (or from) Apple
   The Chinese DE constructions are also often translated into prepositions in English.

cc* and *punct The Chinese sentences contain more punctuation (*punct*) while the English translation has more conjunctions (*cc*), because English uses conjunctions to link clauses ("and" in (6b)) while Chinese tends to use only punctuation ("," in (6a)).

(6a) 这些/these 城市/city 社会/social 经济/economic 发展/development 迅速/rapid ， 地方/local 经济/economic 实力/strength 明显/clearly 增强/enhance
(6b) In these municipalities the social and economic development has been rapid, and the local economic strength has clearly been enhanced

rcmod* and *ccomp There are more *rcmod* and *ccomp* in the Chinese sentences and less in the English translation, because of the following reasons:

1. Some English adjectives act as verbs in Chinese. For example, 新 (new) is an adjectival predicate in Chinese and the relation between 新 (new) and 制度 (system) is *rcmod*. But "new" is an adjective in English and the English relation between "new" and "system" is *amod*. This difference contributes to more *rcmod* in Chinese.
   (7a) 新/new 的/(DE) 核销/verify and write off
   (7b) a new sales verification system
2. Chinese has two special verbs (VC): 是 (SHI) and 为 (WEI) which English doesn't use. For

abbreviation	short description	Chinese example	typed dependency	counts	percentage
nn	noun compound modifier	服务 中心	nn(中心, 服务)	13278	15.48%
punct	punctuation	海关 统计 表明 ,	punct(表明, ,)	10896	12.71%
nsubj	nominal subject	梅花 盛开	nsubj(盛开, 梅花)	5893	6.87%
conj	conjunct (links two conjuncts)	设备 和 原材料	conj(原材料, 设备)	5438	6.34%
dobj	direct object	浦东 颁布 了 七十一 件 文件	dobj(颁布, 文件)	5221	6.09%
advmod	adverbial modifier	部门 先 送上 文件	advmod(送上, 先)	4231	4.93%
prep	prepositional modifier	在 实践 中 逐步 完善	prep(完善, 在)	3138	3.66%
nummod	number modifier	七十一 件 文件	nummod(件, 七十一)	2885	3.36%
amod	adjectival modifier	跨世纪 工程	amod(工程, 跨世纪)	2691	3.14%
pobj	prepositional object	根据 有关 规定	pobj(根据, 规定)	2417	2.82%
rcmod	relative clause modifier	不 曾 遇到 过 的 情况	rcmod(情况, 遇到)	2348	2.74%
cpm	complementizer	开发 浦东 的 经济 活动	cpm(开发, 的)	2013	2.35%
assm	associative marker	企业 的 商品	assm(企业, 的)	1969	2.30%
assmod	associative modifier	企业 的 商品	assmod(商品, 企业)	1941	2.26%
cc	coordinating conjunction	设备 和 原材料	cc(原材料, 和)	1763	2.06%
clf	classifier modifier	七十一 件 文件	clf(文件, 件)	1558	1.82%
ccomp	clausal complement	银行 决定 先 取得 信用 评级	ccomp(决定, 取得)	1113	1.30%
det	determiner	这些 经济 活动	det(活动, 这些)	1113	1.30%
lobj	localizer object	近年 来	lobj(来, 近年)	1010	1.18%
range	dative object that is a quantifier phrase	成交 药品 一亿多 元	range(成交, 元)	891	1.04%
asp	aspect marker	发挥 了 作用	asp(发挥, 了)	857	1.00%
tmod	temporal modifier	以前 不 曾 遇到 过	tmod(遇到, 以前)	679	0.79%
plmod	localizer modifier of a preposition	在 这 片 热土 上	plmod(在, 上)	630	0.73%
attr	attributive	贸易额 为 二百亿 美元	attr(为, 美元)	534	0.62%
mmod	modal verb modifier	利益 能 得到 保障	mmod(得到, 能)	497	0.58%
loc	localizer	占 九成 以上	loc(占, 以上)	428	0.50%
top	topic	建筑 是 主要 活动	top(是, 建筑)	380	0.44%
pccomp	clausal complement of a preposition	据 有关 部门 介绍	pccomp(据, 介绍)	374	0.44%
etc	etc modifier	科技 、 文教 等 领域	etc(文教, 等)	295	0.34%
lccomp	clausal complement of a localizer	中国 对 外 开放 中 升起 的 明星	lccomp(中, 开放)	207	0.24%
ordmod	ordinal number modifier	第七 个 机构	ordmod(个, 第七)	199	0.23%
xsubj	controlling subject	银行 决定 先 取得 信用 评级	xsubj(取得, 银行)	192	0.22%
neg	negative modifier	以前 不 曾 遇到 过	neg(遇到, 不)	186	0.22%
rcomp	resultative complement	研究 成功	rcomp(研究, 成功)	176	0.21%
comod	coordinated verb compound modifier	颁布 实行	comod(颁布, 实行)	150	0.17%
vmod	verb modifier	其 在 支持 外商 企业 方面 的 作用	vmod(方面, 支持)	133	0.16%
prtmod	particles such as 所, 以, 来, 而	在 产业化 所 取得 的 成就	prtmod(取得, 所)	124	0.14%
ba	"ba" construction	把 注意力 转向 市场	ba(转向, 把)	95	0.11%
dvpm	manner DE(地) modifier	有效 地 防止 流失	dvpm(有效, 地)	73	0.09%
dvpmod	a "XP+DEV(地)" phrase that modifies VP	有效 地 防止 流失	dvpmod(防止, 有效)	69	0.08%
prnmod	parenthetical modifier	八五 期间 （ 1990 – 1995 ）	prnmod(期间, 1995)	67	0.08%
cop	copular	原 是 自给自足 的 经济	cop(自给自足, 是)	59	0.07%
pass	passive marker	被 认定 为 高 技术 产业	pass(认定, 被)	53	0.06%
nsubjpass	nominal passive subject	镍 被 称作 现代 工业 的 维生素	nsubjpass(称作, 镍)	14	0.02%

Table 2: Chinese grammatical relations and examples. The counts are from files 1–325 in CTB6.

example, there is an additional relation, *ccomp*, between the verb 是/(SHI) and 降低/reduce in (8a). The relation is not necessary in English, since 是/SHI is not translated.

(8a) 二/second 是/(SHI) 一九九六年/1996 中国/China 大幅度/substantially 降低/reduce 关税/tariff

(8b) Second, China reduced tax substantially in 1996.

conj There are more *conj* in Chinese than in English for three major reasons. First, sometimes one complete Chinese sentence is translated into several English sentences. Our *conj* is defined for two grammatical roles occurring in the same sentence, and therefore, when a sentence breaks into multiple ones, the original relation does not apply. Second, we define the two grammatical roles linked by the *conj* relation to be in the same word class. However, words which are in the same word class in Chinese may not be in the same word class in English. For example, adjective predicates act as verbs in Chinese, but as adjectives in English. Third, certain constructions with two verbs are described differently between the two languages: verb pairs are described as coordinations in a serial verb construction in Chinese, but as the second verb being the complement of the first verb in English.

4 Experimental Results

4.1 Experimental Setting

We use various Chinese-English parallel corpora[1] for both training the phrase orientation classifier, and for extracting statistical phrases for the phrase-based MT system. The parallel data contains 1,560,071 sentence pairs from various parallel corpora. There are 12,259,997 words on the English side. Chinese word segmentation is done by the Stanford Chinese segmenter (Chang et al., 2008). After segmentation, there are 11,061,792 words on the Chinese side. The alignment is done by the Berkeley word aligner (Liang et al., 2006) and then we symmetrized the word alignment using the grow-diag heuristic.

For the phrase orientation classifier experiments, we extracted labeled examples using the parallel data and the alignment as in Figure 2. We extracted 9,194,193 total valid examples: 86.09% of them are *ordered* and the other 13.91% are *reversed*. To evaluate the classifier performance, we split these examples into training, dev and test set (8 : 1 : 1). The phrase orientation classifier used in MT experiments is trained with all of the available labeled examples.

Our MT experiments use a re-implementation of Moses (Koehn et al., 2003) called *Phrasal*, which provides an easier API for adding features. We use a 5-gram language model trained on the Xinhua and AFP sections of the Gigaword corpus (LDC2007T40) and also the English side of all the LDC parallel data permissible under the NIST08 rules. Documents of Gigaword released during the epochs of MT02, MT03, MT05, and MT06 were removed. For features in MT experiments, we incorporate Moses' standard eight features as well as the lexicalized reordering features. To have a more comparable setting with (Zens and Ney, 2006), we also have a baseline experiment with only the standard eight features. Parameter tuning is done with Minimum Error Rate Training (MERT) (Och, 2003). The tuning set for MERT is the NIST MT06 data set, which includes 1664 sentences. We evaluate the result with MT02 (878 sentences), MT03 (919 sentences), and MT05 (1082 sentences).

[1]LDC2002E18, LDC2003E07, LDC2003E14, LDC2005E83, LDC2005T06, LDC2006E26, LDC2006E85, LDC2002L27 and LDC2005T34.

4.2 Phrase Orientation Classifier

Feature Sets	#features	Train. Acc. (%)	Train. Macro-F	Dev Acc. (%)	Dev Macro-F
Majority class	-	86.09	-	86.09	-
Src	1483696	89.02	71.33	88.14	69.03
Src+Tgt	2976108	92.47	82.52	91.29	79.80
Src+Src2+Tgt	4440492	95.03	88.76	93.64	85.58
Src+Src2+Tgt+PATH	4691887	96.01	91.15	94.27	87.22

Table 3: Feature engineering of the phrase orientation classifier. Accuracy is defined as (#correctly labeled examples) divided by (#all examples). The macro-F is an average of the accuracies of the two classes.

The basic source word features described in Section 2 are referred to as Src, and the target word features as Tgt. The feature set that Zens and Ney (2006) used in their MT experiments is Src+Tgt. In addition to that, we also experimented with source word features Src2 which are similar to Src, but take a window of 3 around j' instead of j. In Table 3 we can see that adding the Src2 features increased the total number of features by almost 50%, but also improved the performance. The PATH features add fewer total number of features than the lexical features, but still provide a 10% error reduction and 1.63 on the macro-F1 on the dev set. We use the best feature sets from the feature engineering in Table 3 and test it on the test set. We get 94.28% accuracy and 87.17 macro-F1. The overall improvement of accuracy over the baseline is 8.19 absolute points.

4.3 MT Experiments

In the MT setting, we use the log probability from the phrase orientation classifier as an extra feature. The weight of this discriminative reordering feature is also tuned by MERT, along with other Moses features. In order to understand how much the PATH features add value to the MT experiments, we trained two phrase orientation classifiers with different features: one with the Src+Src2+Tgt feature set, and the other one with Src+Src2+Tgt+PATH. The results are listed in Table 4. We compared to two different baselines: one is Moses8Features which has a distance-based reordering model, the other is Baseline which also includes lexicalized reordering features. From the table we can see that using the discriminative reordering model with PATH features gives significant improvement over both base-

Setting	#MERT features	MT06(tune)	MT02	MT03	MT05
Moses8Features	8	31.49	31.63	31.26	30.26
Moses8Features+DiscrimRereorderNoPATH	9	31.76(+0.27)	31.86(+0.23)	**32.09**(+**0.83**)	**31.14**(+**0.88**)
Moses8Features+DiscrimRereorderWithPATH	9	**32.34**(+**0.85**)	**32.59**(+**0.96**)	**32.70**(+**1.44**)	**31.84**(+**1.58**)
Baseline (Moses with lexicalized reordering)	16	32.55	32.56	32.65	31.89
Baseline+DiscrimRereorderNoPATH	17	32.73(+0.18)	32.58(+0.02)	32.99(+0.34)	31.80(−0.09)
Baseline+DiscrimRereorderWithPATH	17	**32.97**(+**0.42**)	**33.15**(+**0.59**)	**33.65**(+**1.00**)	**32.66**(+**0.77**)

Table 4: MT experiments of different settings on various NIST MT evaluation datasets. All differences marked in bold are significant at the level of 0.05 with the approximate randomization test in (Riezler and Maxwell, 2005).

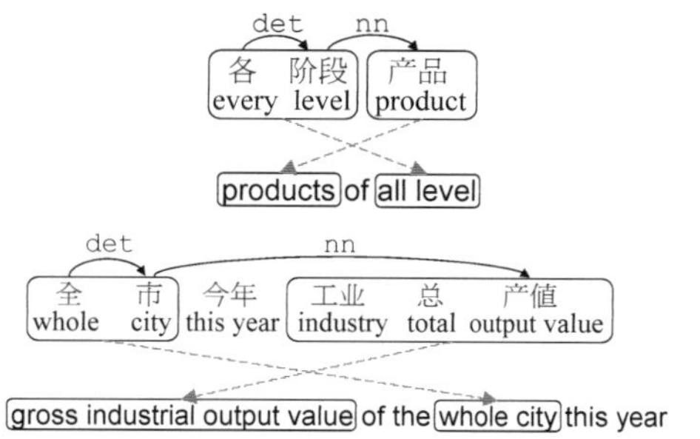

Figure 4: Two examples for the feature *PATH:det-nn* and how the reordering occurs.

lines. If we use the discriminative reordering model without PATH features and only with word features, we still get improvement over the Moses8Features baseline, but the MT performance is not significantly different from Baseline which uses lexicalized reordering features. From Table 4 we see that using the Src+Src2+Tgt+PATH features significantly outperforms both baselines. Also, if we compare between Src+Src2+Tgt and Src+Src2+Tgt+PATH, the differences are also statistically significant, which shows the effectiveness of the path features.

4.4 Analysis: Highly-weighted Features in the Phrase Orientation Model

There are a lot of features in the log-linear phrase orientation model. We looked at some highly-weighted PATH features to understand what kind of grammatical constructions were informative for phrase orientation. We found that many path features corresponded to our intuitions. For example, the feature *PATH:prep-dobjR* has a high weight for being *reversed*. This feature informs the model that in Chinese a PP usually appears before VP, but in English they should be reversed. Other features with high weights include features related to the DE construction that is more likely to translate to a relative clause, such as *PATH:advmod-rcmod* and *PATH:rcmod*. They also indicate the phrases are more likely to be chosen in reversed order. Another frequent pattern that has not been emphasized in the previous literature is *PATH:det-nn*, meaning that a [DT NP_1NP_2] in Chinese is translated into English as [NP_2 DT NP_1]. Examples with this feature are in Figure 4. We can see that the important features decided by the phrase orientation model are also important from a linguistic perspective.

5 Conclusion

We introduced a set of Chinese typed dependencies that gives information about grammatical relations between words, and which may be useful in other NLP applications as well as MT. We used the typed dependencies to build path features and used them to improve a phrase orientation classifier. The path features gave a 10% error reduction on the accuracy of the classifier and 1.63 points on the macro-F1 score. We applied the log probability as an additional feature in a phrase-based MT system, which improved the BLEU score of the three test sets significantly (0.59 on MT02, 1.00 on MT03 and 0.77 on MT05). This shows that typed dependencies on the source side are informative for the reordering component in a phrase-based system. Whether typed dependencies can lead to improvements in other syntax-based MT systems remains a question for future research.

Acknowledgments

The authors would like to thank Marie-Catherine de Marneffe for her help on the typed dependencies, and Daniel Cer for building the decoder. This work is funded by a Stanford Graduate Fellowship to the first author and gift funding from Google for the project "Translating Chinese Correctly".

References

Pi-Chuan Chang, Michel Galley, and Christopher D. Manning. 2008. Optimizing Chinese word segmentation for machine translation performance. In *Proceedings of the Third Workshop on Statistical Machine Translation*, pages 224–232, Columbus, Ohio, June. Association for Computational Linguistics.

Marie-Catherine de Marneffe and Christopher D. Manning. 2008. The Stanford typed dependencies representation. In *Coling 2008: Proceedings of the workshop on Cross-Framework and Cross-Domain Parser Evaluation*, pages 1–8, Manchester, UK, August. Coling 2008 Organizing Committee.

Marie-Catherine de Marneffe, Bill MacCartney, and Christopher D. Manning. 2006. Generating typed dependency parses from phrase structure parses. In *Proceedings of LREC-06*, pages 449–454.

Liang Huang, Kevin Knight, and Aravind Joshi. 2006. Statistical syntax-directed translation with extended domain of locality. In *Proceedings of AMTA*, Boston, MA.

Philipp Koehn, Franz Josef Och, and Daniel Marcu. 2003. Statistical phrase-based translation. In *Proc. of NAACL-HLT*.

Philipp Koehn, Hieu Hoang, Alexandra Birch Mayne, Christopher Callison-Burch, Marcello Federico, Nicola Bertoldi, Brooke Cowan, Wade Shen, Christine Moran, Richard Zens, Chris Dyer, Ondrej Bojar, Alexandra Constantin, and Evan Herbst. 2007. Moses: Open source toolkit for statistical machine translation. In *Proceedings of the 45th Annual Meeting of the Association for Computational Linguistics (ACL), Demonstration Session.*

Percy Liang, Ben Taskar, and Dan Klein. 2006. Alignment by agreement. In *Proceedings of HLT-NAACL*, pages 104–111, New York City, USA, June. Association for Computational Linguistics.

Franz Josef Och, Daniel Gildea, Sanjeev Khudanpur, Anoop Sarkar, Kenji Yamada, Alex Fraser, Shankar Kumar, Libin Shen, David Smith, Katherine Eng, Viren Jain, Zhen Jin, and Dragomir Radev. 2004. A smorgasbord of features for statistical machine translation. In *Proceedings of HLT-NAACL*.

Franz Josef Och. 2003. Minimum error rate training for statistical machine translation. In *ACL*.

Stefan Riezler and John T. Maxwell. 2005. On some pitfalls in automatic evaluation and significance testing for MT. In *Proceedings of the ACL Workshop on Intrinsic and Extrinsic Evaluation Measures for Machine Translation and/or Summarization*, pages 57–64, Ann Arbor, Michigan, June. Association for Computational Linguistics.

Christoph Tillman. 2004. A unigram orientation model for statistical machine translation. In *Proceedings of HLT-NAACL 2004: Short Papers*, pages 101–104.

Chao Wang, Michael Collins, and Philipp Koehn. 2007. Chinese syntactic reordering for statistical machine translation. In *Proceedings of the 2007 Joint Conference on Empirical Methods in Natural Language Processing and Computational Natural Language Learning (EMNLP-CoNLL)*, pages 737–745, Prague, Czech Republic, June. Association for Computational Linguistics.

Richard Zens and Hermann Ney. 2006. Discriminative reordering models for statistical machine translation. In *Proceedings on the Workshop on Statistical Machine Translation*, pages 55–63, New York City, June. Association for Computational Linguistics.

On the complexity of alignment problems in two synchronous grammar formalisms

Anders Søgaard*
Center for Language Technology
University of Copenhagen
soegaard@hum.ku.dk

Abstract

The alignment problem for synchronous grammars in its unrestricted form, i.e. whether for a grammar and a string pair the grammar induces an alignment of the two strings, reduces to the universal recognition problem, but restrictions may be imposed on the alignment sought, e.g. alignments may be $1:1$, island-free or sure-possible sorted. The complexities of 15 restricted alignment problems in two very different synchronous grammar formalisms of syntax-based machine translation, inversion transduction grammars (ITGs) (Wu, 1997) and a restricted form of range concatenation grammars ((2,2)-BRCGs) (Søgaard, 2008), are investigated. The universal recognition problems, and therefore also the unrestricted alignment problems, of both formalisms can be solved in time $\mathcal{O}(n^6|G|)$. The complexities of the restricted alignment problems differ significantly, however.

1 Introduction

The synchronous grammar formalisms used in syntax-based machine translation typically induce alignments by aligning all words that are recognized simultaneously (Wu, 1997; Zhang and Gildea, 2004). On a par with weak and strong generative capacity, it is thus possible to talk about the alignment capacity of those formalisms. In this paper, two synchronous grammar formalisms are discussed, inversion transduction grammars (ITGs) (Wu, 1997) and two-variable binary bottom-up non-erasing range concatenation grammars ((2,2)-BRCGs) (Søgaard, 2008). It is known that ITGs do not induce the class of inside-out alignments discussed in Wu (1997). Another class that ITGs do not induce is that of alignments with discontinuous translation units (Søgaard, 2008). Søgaard (2008), on the other hand, shows that the alignments induced by (2,2)-BRCGs are closed under union, i.e. (2,2)-BRCGs induce all possible alignments.

The universal recognition problems of both ITGs and (2,2)-BRCGs can be solved in time $\mathcal{O}(n^6|G|)$. This may come as a surprise, as ITGs restrict the alignment search space considerably, while (2,2)-BRCGs do not. In the context of the NP-hardness of decoding in statistical machine translation (Knight, 1999; Udupa and Maji, 2006), it is natural to ask why the universal recognition problem of (2,2)-BRCGs isn't NP-hard? How can (2,2)-BRCGs induce all possible alignments and still avoid NP-hardness? This paper bridges the gap between these results and shows that when alignments are restricted to be $1:1$, island-free or sure-possible sorted (see below), or all combinations thereof, the alignment problem of (2,2)-BRCGs *is* NP-hard. (2,2)-BRCGs in a sense avoid NP-hardness by giving up control over global properties of alignments, e.g. any pair of words may be aligned multiple times in a derivation.

*This work was done while the first author was a Senior Researcher at the Dpt. of Linguistics, University of Potsdam, supported by the German Research Foundation in the Emmy Noether project *Ptolemaios* on grammar learning from parallel corpora; and while he was a Postdoctoral Researcher at the ISV Computational Linguistics Group, Copenhagen Business School, supported by the Danish Research Foundation in the project *Efficient syntax- and semantics-based machine translation*.

Proceedings of SSST-3, Third Workshop on Syntax and Structure in Statistical Translation, pages 60–68,
Boulder, Colorado, June 2009.

The alignment structures induced by synchronous grammars in syntax-based machine translation have the following property: If an alignment structure includes alignments $v|v'$, $v|w'$ and $w|w'$, it also includes the alignment $w|v'$, where w, w', v, v' are word instances.[1] This follows from the fact that only words that are recognized simultanously, are aligned. Otherwise alignment structures are just a binary symmetric relation on two strings, a source and a target string, such that two words in the source, resp. target string, cannot be aligned. Maximally connected subgraphs (ignoring precedence edges) are called translation units.

The alignment problem can be formulated this way (with s, s' source and target sentence, resp.):

INSTANCE:	$G, \langle s, s' \rangle$.
QUESTION:	Does G induce an alignment on $\langle s, s' \rangle$?

The alignment problem in its unrestricted form reduces to the universal recognition problem (Barton et al., 1987), i.e. whether for a grammar G and a string pair $\langle s, s' \rangle$ it holds that $\langle s, s' \rangle \in L(G)$? Of course the alignment may in this case be empty or partial. Both ITGs and (2,2)-BRCGs permit unaligned nodes.

This paper investigates the complexity of restricted versions of the alignment problem for ITGs and (2,2)-BRCGs. A simple example, which can be solved in linear time for both formalisms, is the alignment problem wrt. alignments that consist of a single translation unit including all source and target words. It may be formulated this way:

INSTANCE:	$G, \langle s, s' \rangle$.
QUESTION:	Does G induce an alignment that consists of a single translation unit with no unaligned words on $\langle s, s' \rangle$?

This can be solved for ITGs by checking if there is a production rule that introduces all the words in the right order such that:[2]

- The LHS nonterminal symbol (possibly suffixed by the empty string ϵ) can be derived from the start symbol.
- The empty string ϵ can be derived from all RHS nonterminal symbols.

The only difference for (2,2)-BRCGs is that production rules are typically referred to as clauses in the range concatenation grammar literature.

This paper considers some more complex examples; namely, the alignment problems wrt. $1:1$-alignments, (source-side and/or target-side) island-free alignments and sure-possible sorted alignments. The formal definitions of the three properties are as follows:

Definition 1.1. An alignment structure for a string pair $\langle w_1 \dots w_n, v_1 \dots v_m \rangle$ is a graph $D = \langle V, E \rangle$ where $V = V_s : \{w_1, \dots, w_n\} \cup V_t : \{v_1, \dots, v_m\}$ and $E = E_s : \{w_i \prec w_j \mid i < j\} \cup E_t : \{v_i \prec v_j \mid i < j\} \cup A$ where $A \subseteq V_s \times V_t$. If $(w_i, v_j) \in A$, also written $w_i|v_j$, w_i is said to be aligned to v_j, and vice versa. An alignment structure is said to be *wellformed* iff for all $w_i, w_j, v_{i'}, v_{j'}$ it holds that if $w_i|v_{i'}, w_i|v_{j'}$ and $w_j|v_{i'}$ are aligned then so are $w_j|v_{j'}$. An alignment structure is said to be $1:1$ iff no word occurs in two distinct tuples in A. An alignment structure is said to be *island-free* iff all words in V occur in some tuple in A; it is said to be source-side, resp. target-side, island-free if all words in V_s, resp. V_t, occur in some tuple in A. The set of alignments is divided into sure and possible alignments, i.e. $A = S \cup P$ (in most cases $P = \emptyset$). An alignment structure is said to be *sure-possible sorted* iff if it holds that $(w_i, v_{j'}) \in S$ then for all $w_j, v_{i'}$ neither $(w_i, v_{i'}) \in P$ nor $(w_j, v_{j'}) \in P$ holds; similarly, if it holds that $(w_i, v_{j'}) \in P$ then for all $w_j, v_{i'}$ neither $(w_i, v_{i'}) \in S$ nor $(w_j, v_{j'}) \in S$ holds.

The precedence relations in E are not important for any of our definitions, but are important for meaningful interpretation of alignment structures. Note that synchronous grammars are guaranteed to induce wellformed alignment structures. Some brief motivation for the properties singled out:

[1] $w|w'$ is our short hand notation for saying that w, a word in the source string, and w', a word in the target string, have been aligned. In the formal definition of alignments below, it is said that $w \in V_s$ (w is a word in the source string), $w' \in V_t$ (w' is a word in the target string) and $(w, w') \in A$, i.e. w is aligned to w', and vice versa. Alignments are bidirectional in what follows.

[2] In fact in normal form ITGs, we can simply check if there is a production rule with the start symbol in the LHS that introduces all the words in the right order, since all production rules with nonterminal symbols in the RHS are branching and contain no terminal symbols.

Result	1 : 1	IF(s)	IF(t)	SP	ITGs	(2,2)-BRCGs
(1)	✓				$\mathcal{O}(n^6\|G\|)$	NP-complete
(2)		✓			$\mathcal{O}(n^6\|G\|)$	NP-complete
(3)			✓		$\mathcal{O}(n^6\|G\|)$	NP-complete
(4)				✓	$\mathcal{O}(n^6\|G\|)$	NP-complete
(5)	✓	✓			$\mathcal{O}(n^6\|G\|)$	NP-complete
(6)		✓	✓		$\mathcal{O}(n^6\|G\|)$	NP-complete
(7)			✓	✓	$\mathcal{O}(n^6\|G\|)$	NP-complete
(8)	✓		✓		$\mathcal{O}(n^6\|G\|)$	NP-complete
(9)		✓		✓	$\mathcal{O}(n^6\|G\|)$	NP-complete
(10)	✓			✓	$\mathcal{O}(n^6\|G\|)$	NP-complete
(11)	✓	✓	✓		$\mathcal{O}(n^6\|G\|)$	NP-complete
(12)		✓	✓	✓	$\mathcal{O}(n^6\|G\|)$	NP-complete
(13)	✓		✓	✓	$\mathcal{O}(n^6\|G\|)$	NP-complete
(14)	✓	✓		✓	$\mathcal{O}(n^6\|G\|)$	NP-complete
(15)	✓	✓	✓	✓	$\mathcal{O}(n^6\|G\|)$	NP-complete

Figure 1: The complexity of restricted alignment problems for ITGs and (2,2)-BRCGs.

- $1:1$-alignments have been argued to be adequate by Melamed (1999) and elsewhere, and it may therefore be useful to know if a grammar extracted from a parallel corpus produces $1:1$-alignments for a finite set of sentence pairs.
- Island-free alignments are interesting to the extent that unaligned nodes increase the chance of translation errors. An island threshold may for instance be used to rule out risky translations.
- The notion of sure-possible sorted alignments is more unusual, but can, for instance, be used to check if the use of possible alignments is consistently triggered by words that are hard to align.

The results for all cross-classifications of the four properties – $1:1$, source-side island-free (IF(s)), target-side island-free (IF(t)) and sure-possible sorted (SP) – are presented in the table in Figure 1.[3] Note that all ($2^4 - 1 = 15$) combinations of the four properties lead to NP-hard alignment problems for (2,2)-BRCGs. Consequently, while the unrestricted alignment problem for (2,2)-BRCGs can be solved in $\mathcal{O}(n^6|G|)$, the alignment problem turns NP-hard as soon as restrictions are put on the alignments sought. So the extra expressivity of (2,2)-BRCGs in a way comes at the expense of control over the kind of alignments obtained.

On the structure of the paper: Sect. 2 and 3 briefly introduce, resp., ITGs and (2,2)-BRCGs. Sect. 4 presents three NP-hardness proofs from which the 15 results in Figure 1 can be derived. The three proofs are based on reconstructions of the Hamilton circuit problem, the 3SAT problem and the vertex cover problem (Garey and Johnson, 1979).

[3] One of our reviewers remarks that the Figure 1 is 'artificially blown up', since all combinations have the same complexity. It cannot really be left out, however. The numbers in the figure's left-most column serves as a reference in the proofs below. Since the 15 results derive from only four proofs, it is convenient to have a short-hand notation for the decision problems.

2 Inversion transduction grammars

Inversion transduction grammars (ITGs) (Wu, 1997) are a notational variant of binary syntax-directed translation schemas (Aho and Ullman, 1972) and are usually presented with a normal form:

$$\begin{array}{lcl} A & \rightarrow & [BC] \\ A & \rightarrow & \langle BC \rangle \\ A & \rightarrow & e \mid f \\ A & \rightarrow & e \mid \epsilon \\ A & \rightarrow & \epsilon \mid f \end{array}$$

where $A, B, C \in N$ and $e, f \in T$. The first production rule, intuitively, says that the subtree $[[]_B[]_C]_A$ in the source language translates into a subtree $[[]_B[]_C]_A$, whereas the second production rule inverts the order in the target language, i.e. $[[]_C[]_B]_A$. The universal recognition problem of ITGs can be solved in time $\mathcal{O}(n^6|G|)$ by a CYK-style parsing algorithm with two charts.

Figure 1 tells us that all the restricted alignment problems listed can be solved in time $\mathcal{O}(n^6|G|)$. The explanation is simple. It can be read off from the syntactic form of the production rules in ITGs whether they introduce $1:1$-alignments, island-free alignments or sure-possible sorted alignments. Note that normal form ITGs only induce $1:1$-alignments.

Consider, for example, the following grammar, not in normal form for brevity:

$$\begin{array}{llll} (1) & S & \rightarrow & \langle ASB \rangle \mid \langle AB \rangle \\ (2) & A & \rightarrow & a \mid a \\ (3) & A & \rightarrow & a \mid \epsilon \\ (4) & B & \rightarrow & b \mid b \end{array}$$

Note that this grammar recognizes the translation $\{\langle a^n b^n, b^n a^m \mid n \geq m\}$. To check if for a string pair $\langle w_1 \dots w_n, v_1 \dots v_m \rangle$ this grammar induces an island-free alignment, simply remove production rule (3). It holds that only strings in the sub-language $\{\langle a^n b^n, b^n a^n \mid n \geq 1\}$ induce island-free alignments. Similarly, to check if the grammar induces source-side island-free alignments for string pairs, no production rules will have to be removed.

3 Two-variable binary bottom-up non-erasing range concatenation grammars

(2,2)-BRCGs are *positive* RCGs (Boullier, 1998) with binary start predicate names, i.e. $\rho(S) = 2$. In RCG, predicates can be negated (for complementation), and the start predicate name is typically unary. The definition is changed only for aesthetic reasons; a positive RCG with a binary start predicate name S is turned into a positive RCG with a unary start predicate name S' simply by adding a clause $S'(X_1X_2) \rightarrow S(X_1, X_2)$.

A positive RCG is a 5-tuple $G = \langle N, T, V, P, S \rangle$. N is a finite set of predicate names with an arity function ρ: $N \rightarrow \mathbb{N}$, T and V are finite sets of, resp., terminal and variables. P is a finite set of clauses of the form $\psi_0 \rightarrow \psi_1 \dots \psi_m$, where each of the $\psi_i, 0 \leq i \leq m$, is a predicate of the form $A(\alpha_1, \dots, \alpha_{\rho(A)})$. Each $\alpha_j \in (T \cup V)^*, 1 \leq j \leq \rho(A)$, is an argument. $S \in N$ is the start predicate name with $\rho(S) = 2$.

Note that the order of RHS predicates in a clause is of no importance. Three subclasses of RCGs are introduced for further reference: An RCG $G = \langle N, T, V, P, S \rangle$ is *simple* iff for all $c \in P$, it holds that no variable X occurs more than once in the LHS of c, and if X occurs in the LHS then it occurs exactly once in the RHS, and each argument in the RHS of c contains exactly one variable. An RCG $G = \langle N, T, V, P, S \rangle$ is a *k-RCG* iff for all $A \in N, \rho(A) \leq k$. Finally, an RCG $G = \langle N, T, V, P, S \rangle$ is said to be *bottom-up non-erasing* iff for all $c \in P$ all variables that occur in the RHS of c also occur in its LHS.

A positive RCG is a (2,2)-BRCG iff it is a 2-RCG, if an argument of the LHS predicate contains at most two variables, and if it is bottom-up non-erasing.

The language of a (2,2)-BRCG is based on the notion of *range*. For a string pair $\langle w_1 \dots w_n, v_{n+2} \dots v_{n+1+m} \rangle$ a range is a pair of indices $\langle i, j \rangle$ with $0 \leq i \leq j \leq n$ or $n < i \leq j \leq n + 1 + m$, i.e. a string span, which denotes a substring $w_{i+1} \dots w_j$ in the source string or a substring $v_{i+1} \dots v_j$ in the target string. Only consequtive ranges can be concatenated into new ranges. Terminals, variables and arguments in a clause are bound to ranges by a substitution mechanism. An *instantiated* clause is a clause in which variables and arguments are consistently replaced by ranges; its components are *instantiated predicates*. For example $A(\langle g \dots h \rangle, \langle i \dots j \rangle) \rightarrow B(\langle g \dots h \rangle, \langle i+1 \dots j-1 \rangle)$ is an instantiation of the clause $A(X_1, aY_1b) \rightarrow B(X_1, Y_1)$ if the target string is such that $v_{i+1} = a$ and $v_j = b$. A *derive* relation $\Longrightarrow$ is defined on strings of instantiated predicates. If an instantiated predicate is the LHS of some instantiated clause, it can be replaced by the RHS of that instantiated clause. The language of a (2,2)-BRCG $G = \langle N, T, V, P, S \rangle$ is the set $L(G) = \{\langle w_1 \dots w_n, v_{n+2} \dots v_{n+1+m} \rangle \mid S(\langle 0, n \rangle, \langle n+1, n+1+m \rangle) \stackrel{*}{\Longrightarrow} \epsilon\}$, i.e. an input string pair $\langle w_1 \dots w_n, v_{n+2} \dots v_{n+1+m} \rangle$ is recognized iff the empty string can be derived from $S(\langle 0, n \rangle, \langle n+1, n+1+m \rangle)$.

It is not difficult to see that ITGs are also (2,2)-BRCGs. The left column is ITG production rules;

the right column their translations in simple (2,2)-BRCGs.

$A \rightarrow [BC]$	$A(X_1X_2, Y_1Y_2) \rightarrow B(X_1, Y_1)C(X_2, Y_2)$
$A \rightarrow \langle BC \rangle$	$A(X_1X_2, Y_1Y_2) \rightarrow B(X_1, Y_2)C(X_2, Y_1)$
$A \rightarrow e \mid f$	$A(e, f) \rightarrow \epsilon$
$A \rightarrow e \mid \epsilon$	$A(e, \epsilon) \rightarrow \epsilon$
$A \rightarrow \epsilon \mid f$	$A(\epsilon, f) \rightarrow \epsilon$

Consequently, (2,2)-BRCGs recognize all translations recognized by ITGs. In fact the inclusion is strict, as shown in Søgaard (2008). The universal recognition problem of (2,2)-BRCGs can be solved in time $\mathcal{O}(n^6|G|)$ by the CYK-style parsing algorithm presented in Søgaard (2008).

Example 3.1. Consider the (2,2)-BRCG $G = \langle \{S_s, S_0, S_0', S_1, S_1', A, B, C, D\}, \{a, b, c, d\}, \{X_1, X_2, Y_1, Y_2\}, P, S_s \rangle$ with P the following set of clauses:

(1)	$S_s(X_1, Y_1)$	$\rightarrow$	$S_0(X_1, Y_1)S_0'(X_1, Y_1)$
(2)	$S_0(X_1X_2, Y_1)$	$\rightarrow$	$S_1(X_1, Y_1)D(X_2)$
(3)	$S_1(aX_1c, abY_1)$	$\rightarrow$	$S_1(X_1, Y_1)$
(4)	$S_1(X_1, Y_1Y_2)$	$\rightarrow$	$B(X_1)C(Y_1)D(Y_2)$
(5)	$S_0'(X_1X_2, Y_1)$	$\rightarrow$	$S_1'(X_2, Y_1)A(X_1)$
(6)	$S_1'(bX_1d, Y_1cd)$	$\rightarrow$	$S_1'(X_1, Y_1)$
(7)	$S_1'(X_1, Y_1Y_2)$	$\rightarrow$	$C(X_1)A(Y_1)B(Y_2)$
(8)	$A(aX_1)$	$\rightarrow$	$A(X_1)$
(9)	$A(\epsilon)$	$\rightarrow$	ϵ
(10)	$B(bX_1)$	$\rightarrow$	$B(X_1)$
(11)	$B(\epsilon)$	$\rightarrow$	ϵ
(12)	$C(cX_1)$	$\rightarrow$	$C(X_1)$
(13)	$C(\epsilon)$	$\rightarrow$	ϵ
(14)	$D(dX_1)$	$\rightarrow$	$D(X_1)$
(15)	$D(\epsilon)$	$\rightarrow$	ϵ

The string pair $\langle abbcdd, abcdcd \rangle$ is derived:

	$S_s(\langle 0,6\rangle, \langle 0,6\rangle)$	
$\Longrightarrow$	$S_0(\langle 0,6\rangle, \langle 0,6\rangle)S_0'(\langle 0,6\rangle, \langle 0,6\rangle)$	(1)
$\Longrightarrow$	$S_1(\langle 0,4\rangle, \langle 0,6\rangle)D(\langle 4,6\rangle)$ $S_0'(\langle 0,6\rangle, \langle 0,6\rangle)$	(2)
$\Longrightarrow$	$S_1(\langle 0,4\rangle, \langle 0,6\rangle)S_0'(\langle 0,6\rangle, \langle 0,6\rangle)$	(14–15)
$\Longrightarrow$	$S_1(\langle 1,3\rangle, \langle 2,6\rangle)S_0'(\langle 0,6\rangle, \langle 0,6\rangle)$	(3)
$\Longrightarrow$	$B(\langle 1,3\rangle)C(\langle 2,4\rangle)D(\langle 4,6\rangle)$ $S_0'(\langle 0,6\rangle, \langle 0,6\rangle)$	(4)
$\Longrightarrow$	$S_0'(\langle 0,6\rangle, \langle 0,6\rangle)$	(10–15)
$\Longrightarrow$	$S_1'(\langle 1,6\rangle, \langle 0,6\rangle)A(\langle 0,1\rangle)$	(5)
$\Longrightarrow$	$S_1'(\langle 1,6\rangle, \langle 0,6\rangle)$	(8–9)
$\Longrightarrow$	$S_1'(\langle 2,5\rangle, \langle 0,4\rangle)$	(6)
$\Longrightarrow$	$S_1'(\langle 3,4\rangle, \langle 0,2\rangle)$	(6)
$\Longrightarrow$	$C(\langle 3,4\rangle)A(\langle 0,1\rangle)B(\langle 1,2\rangle)$	(7)
$\Longrightarrow$	ϵ	(8–13)

Note that $L(G) = \{\langle a^n b^m c^n d^m, (ab)^n (cd)^m \rangle \mid m, n \geq 0\}$.

4 Results

4.1 Checking island-freeness and sure-possible sortedness

One possible way to check for island-freeness and sure-possible sortedness in the context of (2,2)-BRCGs is to augment the CYK-style algorithm with feature structures (Boolean vectors); all there is needed, e.g. to check sure-possible sortedness, is to pair up the nonterminals inserted in the cells of the chart with a flat feature structure of the form:

$$\begin{bmatrix} \text{SURE}_1 \ val_1 \\ \vdots \\ \text{SURE}_n \ val_n \end{bmatrix}$$

where n is the length of the source, resp. target, string in the source, resp. target, chart, and $1 \leq i \leq n : val_i \in \{+, -\}$. When a clause applies that induces a sure alignment between a word w_i and some word in the target, resp. source, string, the attribute SURE_i is assigned the value +; if a possible alignment is induced between w_i and another word, the attribute is assigned the value -. This can all be done in constant time. A copying clause now checks if the appropriate nonterminals have been inserted in the cells in question, but also that the associated feature structures unify. This can be done in linear time. Feature structures can be used the same way to record what words have been aligned to check island-freeness. Unfortunately, this technique does not guarantee polynomial runtime. Note that there can be 2^n many distinct feature structures for each nonterminal symbol in a chart. Consequently, whereas the size of a cell in the standard CYK algorithm is bounded by $|N|$, and in synchronous parsing by $|N| \times (2n-1)$,[4] the cells are now of exponential size in the worst case.

The following three sections provide three NP-hardness proofs: The first shows that the alignment

[4]The indices used to check that two nonterminals are derived simultaneously (Søgaard, 2008) mean that it may be necessary within a cell in the source, resp. target, chart to keep track of multiple tuples with the same nonterminals. In the worst case, there is a nonterminal for each span in the target, resp. source, chart, i.e. $2n - 1$ many.

problem wrt. $1:1$-alignments is NP-hard for (2,2)-BRCGs and goes by reduction of the Hamilton circuit problem for directed connected graphs. The second shows that the alignment problem wrt. source- or target-side island-free and sure-possible sorted alignments is NP-hard for (2,2)-BRCGs and goes by 3SAT reduction. The third proof is more general and goes by reduction of the vertex cover problem. All three formal decision problems are discussed in detail in Garey and Johnson (1979). All 15 results in Figure 1 are derived from modifications of these proofs.

4.2 NP-hardness of the $1:1$ restriction for (2,2)-BRCGs

Theorem 4.1. *The alignment problem wrt.* $1:1$*-alignments is NP-hard for (2,2)-BRCGs.*

Proof. An instance of the Hamilton circuit problem for directed connected graphs is simply a directed connected graph $G = \langle V, E \rangle$ and the problem is whether there is a path that visits each vertex exactly once and returns to its starting point? Consider, for instance, the directed connected graph:

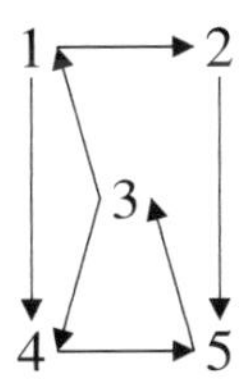

It is easy to see that there is no path in this case that visits each vertex exactly once and returns to its starting point. The intuition behind our reconstruction of the Hamilton circuit problem for directed connected graphs is to check this via alignments between a sequence of all the vertices in the graph and itself. The grammar permits an alignment between two words $w|v$ if there is a directed edge between the corresponding nodes in the graph, e.g. $(w, v) \in E$. The alignment structures below depict the possible alignments induced by the grammar obtained by the translation described below for our example graph:

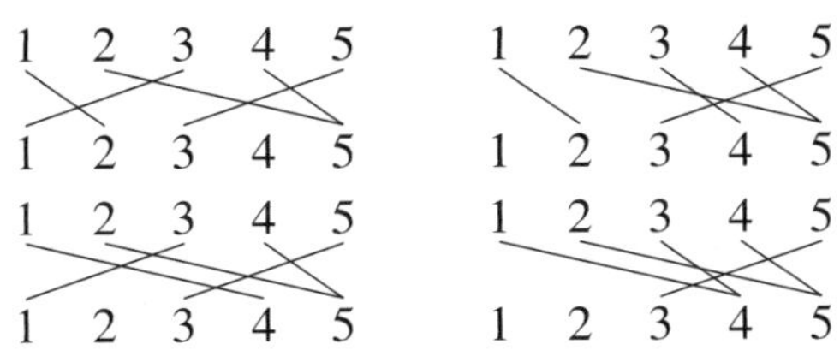

Since no alignment above is $1:1$, there is no solution to the corresponding circuit problem. The translation goes as follows:

- Add a rule $S(X_1, Y_1) \rightarrow \{S_{v_i}(X_1, Y_1) \mid \forall v_i.\exists v_j.(v_i, v_j) \in E\}$.
- For each edge $(v_i, v_j) \in E$ add a rule $S_{v_i}(X_1 v_i X_2, Y_1 v_j Y_2) \rightarrow \top(X_1)\top(X_2)\top(X_3)\top(X_4)$.[5]
- For all $v_i \in V$ add a rule $\top(v_i X_1) \rightarrow \top(X_1)$.
- Add a rule $\top(\epsilon) \rightarrow \epsilon$.

The grammar ensures source-side island-freeness, and therefore if there exists a $1:1$-alignment of any linearization of V and itself, by connectivity of the input graph, there is a solution to the Hamilton circuit problem for directed connected graphs.

□

4.3 NP-hardness of island-freeness and sure-possible sortedness for (2,2)-BRCGs

Theorem 4.2. *The alignment problem wrt. target-side island-free and sure-possible sorted alignments is NP-hard for (2,2)-BRCGs.*

Proof. An instance of the 3SAT problem is a propositional logic formula ϕ that is a conjunction of clauses of three literals connected by disjunctions, and the problem whether this formula is satisfiable, i.e. has a model? Say $\phi = p \vee q \vee r \wedge \bar{p} \vee \bar{q} \vee \bar{r}$. For our reconstruction, we use the propositional variables in ϕ as source string, and ϕ itself with $\wedge$'s omitted and conjuncts as words as the target string. One of the representations of a solution constructed by the translation described below is the following alignment structure:

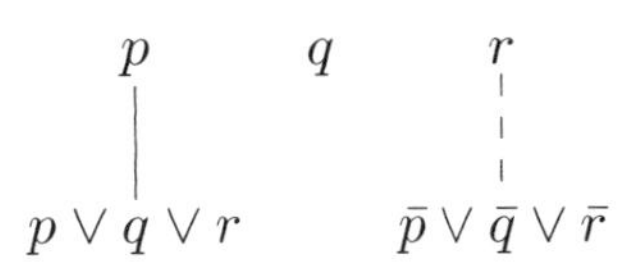

Solid lines are sure alignments; dotted lines are possible alignments. The intuition is to use sure alignments to encode true assignments, and possible alignments as false assignments. The alignment

[5] $\top$ is an arbitrary predicate name chosen to reflect the fact that all possible substrings over the vocabulary are recognized by the $\top$ predicates.

above thus corresponds to the model $\{p, \bar{r}\}$, which clearly satisfies ϕ.

For the translation, assume that each 3SAT instance, over a set of propositional variables $\mathbb{PROP}$, consists of a set of clauses $c_1 \dots c_m$ that are sets of literals of size 3. For any literal l_j, if $l_j = \bar{p_j}$ then $pos(l_j) = p_j$ and $lit(l_j) = -$; and if $l_j = p_j$ then $pos(l_j) = p_j$ and $lit(l_j) = +$. If l_j is a literal in c_i, we write $l_j \in c_i$. First add the following four clauses:

$$\begin{array}{lcl} S_s(X_1,Y_1) & \rightarrow & S_s(X_1,Y_1) \mid S_p(X_1,Y_1) \\ S_p(X_1,Y_1) & \rightarrow & S_s(X_1,Y_1) \mid S_p(X_1,Y_1) \end{array}$$

- If $l_j \in c_i$ and $lit(l_j) = -$, add $S_p(X_1 pos(l_j) X_2, Y_1 c_i Y_2) \rightarrow \top(X_1)\top(X_2)\top(Y_1)\top(Y_2)$.
- If $l_j \in c_i$ and $lit(l_j) = +$, add $S_s(X_1 pos(l_j) X_2, Y_1 c_i Y_2) \rightarrow \top(X_1)\top(X_2)\top(Y_1)\top(Y_2)$.
- For all p_j, add $\top(p_j X_1) \rightarrow \top(X_1)$.
- For all c_i, add $\top(c_i X_1) \rightarrow \top(X_1)$.
- Add a rule $\top(\epsilon) \rightarrow \epsilon$.

It is easy to see that the first rule adds at most $7m$ clauses, which for the largest non-redundant formulas equals $7((2|\mathbb{PROP}|)^3)$. The second rule adds at most $2|\mathbb{PROP}|$ clauses; and the third at most $m \leq (2|\mathbb{PROP}|)^3$ clauses. It is also easy to see that the grammar induces a target-side island-free, sure-possible sorted alignment if and only if the 3SAT instance is satisfiable. Note that the grammar does not guarantee that all induced alignments are target-side island-free. Nothing, in other words, corresponds to conjunctions in our reconstruction. This is not necessary as long as there is at least one target-side island-free alignment that is induced. □

Note that the proof also applies in the case where it is the source side that is required to be island-free. All needed is to make the source string the target string, and vice versa. Note also that the proof can be modified for the case where both sides are island-free: Just add a dummy symbol to the clause side and allow (or force) all propositional variables to be aligned to this dummy symbol. Consequently, if there is a target-side (clause-side) island-free alignment there is also an island-free alignment. Reversely, if there is an island-free alignment there is also a target-side island-free alignment of the string pair in question.

Note also that a more general proof can be obtained by introducing a clause, similar to the clause introduced in the first bullet point of the Hamilton circuit reduction in the proof of Theorem 4.1: $S(X_1,Y_1) \rightarrow \{S_{c_i}(X_1,Y_1) \mid 1 \leq i \leq m\}$. The four rules used to change between sure and possible alignments then of course need to be copied out for all S_{c_i} predicates, and the LHS predicates, except $\top$, of the other clauses must be properly subscripted. Now the grammar enforces target-side island-freeness, and sure-possible sortedness is the only restriction needed on alignments. Consequently, this reduction proves (4) that the alignment problem wrt. sure-possible sortedness is NP-hard for (2,2)-BRCGs.

4.4 NP-hardness of island-freeness for (2,2)-BRCGs

Theorem 4.3. *The alignment problem wrt. island-free alignments is NP-hard for (2,2)-BRCGs.*

Proof. An instance of the vertex problem is a graph $D = \langle V, E\rangle$ and an integer k, and the problem whether there exists a vertex cover of D of size k? Say $D = \langle V = \{a,b,c,d\}, E = \{(a,c),(b,c),(b,d),(c,d)\}\rangle$ and $k = 2$. The translation described below constructs a sentence pair

$$\langle \rho_1\rho_2\rho_3\rho_4 uu\delta\delta\delta\delta, aaaabbbbccccdddd\rangle$$

for this instance, and a (2,2)-BRCG with the clauses in Figure 2. Note that there are four kinds of clauses:

- A clause with an S predicate in the LHS. In general, there will be one such clause in the grammar constructed for any instance of the vertex cover problem.
- 8 clauses with ρ_i predicates in the LHS. In general, there will be $2|E|$ many clauses of this form in the grammars.
- 8 clauses with U^i predicates in the LHS. In general, there will be $|V| \times (|V| - k)$ many clauses of this form in the grammars.

- 16 clauses with δ^1 predicates in the LHS. In general, there will be $(|E| \times |V| - |E| - |E| \times (|V| - k)) \times |V|$ many clauses of this form in the grammars.

For an instance $\langle D = \langle V, E \rangle, k \rangle$, the translation function in general constructs the following clauses:

$$\begin{array}{lll} S(X_1, Y_1) & \rightarrow & \{\rho_i(X_1, Y_1) \mid 1 \leq i \leq |E|\} \cup \\ & & \{U^{|V|-k}(X_1, Y_1)\} \cup \\ & & \{\delta^{|E| \times |V| - |E| - |E| \times (|V|-k)}(X_1, Y_1)\} \end{array}$$

and for all $1 \leq i \leq |E|$ iff $e_i \in E = (e, e')$:

$$\begin{array}{lll} \rho_i(X_1 \rho_i X_2, Y_1 e Y_2) & \rightarrow & \top(X_1)\top(X_2)\top(Y_1)\top(Y_2) \\ \rho_i(X_1 \rho_i X_2, Y_1 e' Y_2) & \rightarrow & \top(X_1)\top(X_2)\top(Y_1)\top(Y_2) \end{array}$$

For all $2 \leq i \leq |V| - k$ and for all $v \in V$:

$$\begin{array}{lll} U^i(X_1 U X_2, Y_1 v \ldots v Y_2) & \rightarrow & U^{i-1}(X_1, Y_1) \\ & & \top(X_2)\top(Y_2) \end{array}$$

where $|v \ldots v| = |E|$. For the case U^1, add the clauses for all $v \in V$:

$$\begin{array}{lll} U^1(X_1 U X_2, Y_1 v \ldots v Y_2) & \rightarrow & \top(X_1)\top(Y_1) \\ & & \top(X_2)\top(Y_2) \end{array}$$

The string pair is constructed this way:

$$\begin{array}{c} \langle \rho_1 \ldots \rho_{|E|} U_1 \ldots U_{|V|-k} \\ \delta_1 \ldots \delta_{|E| \times |V| - |E| - |E| \times (|V|-k)}, \sigma \rangle \end{array}$$

Finally, for all words w in this string pair, add:

$$\top(w X_1) \rightarrow \top(X_1)$$

Since this translation is obviously polynomial, it follows that the alignment problem wrt. island-free alignments for (2,2)-BRCGs is NP-hard. □

Note that the proof also applies if only the source, resp. target, side is required to be island-free, since the grammar restricts the alignments in a way such that if one side is island-free then so is the other side. This gives us results (2) and (3).

It is not difficult to see either that it is possible to convert the grammar into a grammar that induces $1:1$-alignments. This gives us results (5), (8) and (11). Of course by the observation that all the grammars only use sure alignments, it follows that the alignment problems in (7), (9–10) and (12–15) are also NP-hard.

5 Conclusion

The universal recognition problems of both ITGs and (2,2)-BRCGs can be solved in time $\mathcal{O}(n^6|G|)$. This may come as a surprise, as ITGs restrict the alignment space considerably, while (2,2)-BRCGs induce all possible alignments. In the context of the NP-hardness of decoding in statistical machine translation (Knight, 1999; Udupa and Maji, 2006), it is natural to ask why the universal recognition problem of (2,2)-BRCGs isn't NP-hard? This paper bridges the gap between these results and shows that when alignments are restricted to be $1:1$, island-free or sure-possible sorted, or all combinations thereof, the alignment problem of (2,2)-BRCGs *is* NP-hard. Consequently, while the unrestricted alignment problem for (2,2)-BRCGs can be solved in $\mathcal{O}(n^6|G|)$, the alignment problem turns NP-hard as soon as restrictions are put on the alignments sought. So the extra expressivity in a way comes at the expense of control over the kind of alignments obtained. Note also that an alignment of two words may be enforced multiple times in a (2,2)-BRCGs parse, since two derivation trees that share leaves on both sides can align the same two words.

Our results are not intended to be qualifications of the usefulness of (2,2)-BRCGs (Søgaard, 2008), but rather they are attempts to bridge a gap in our understanding of the synchronous grammar formalisms at hand to us in syntax-based machine translation.

$$
\begin{array}{rcl}
S(X_1, Y_1) & \rightarrow & \rho_1(X_1, Y_1)\rho_2(X_1, Y_1) \\
& & \rho_3(X_1, Y_1)\rho_4(X_1, Y_1) \\
& & U^2(X_1, Y_1)\delta^4(X_1, Y_1) \\
\rho_1(X_1\rho_1X_2, Y_1aY_2) & \rightarrow & \top(X_1)\top(X_2)\top(Y_1)\top(Y_2) \\
\rho_1(X_1\rho_1X_2, Y_1cY_2) & \rightarrow & \top(X_1)\top(X_2)\top(Y_1)\top(Y_2) \\
& \ldots & \\
U^2(X_1UX_2, aaaaY_1) & \rightarrow & U^1(X_1, Y_1)\top(X_2) \\
U^1(X_1UX_2, Y_1bbbbY_2) & \rightarrow & \top(X_1)\top(Y_1)\top(X_2)\top(Y_2) \\
U^2(X_1UX_2, Y_1bbbbY_2) & \rightarrow & U^1(X_1, Y_1)\top(X_2)\top(Y_2) \\
& \ldots & \\
\delta^4(X_1\delta X_2, Y_1aY_2) & \rightarrow & \delta^3(X_1, Y_1)\top(X_2)\top(Y_2) \\
\delta^4(X_1\delta X_2, Y_1bY_2) & \rightarrow & \delta^3(X_1, Y_1)\top(X_2)\top(Y_2) \\
& \ldots &
\end{array}
$$

Figure 2: A (2,2)-BRCG for the instance of the vertex cover problem $\langle\langle\{a, b, c, d\}, \{(a, c), (b, c), (b, d), (c, d)\}\rangle, 2\rangle$.

References

Alfred Aho and Jeffrey Ullman. 1972. *The theory of parsing, translation and compiling*. Prentice-Hall, London, England.

Edward Barton, Robert Berwick, and Erik Ristad. 1987. *Computational complexity and natural language*. MIT Press, Cambridge, Massachusetts.

Pierre Boullier. 1998. Proposal for a natural language processing syntactic backbone. Technical report, INRIA, Le Chesnay, France.

Michael Garey and David Johnson. 1979. *Computers and intractability*. W. H. Freeman & Co., New York, New York.

Kevin Knight. 1999. Decoding complexity in word-replacement translation models. *Computational Linguistics*, 25(4):607–615.

Dan Melamed. 1999. Bitext maps and alignment via pattern recognition. *Computational Linguistics*, 25(1):107–130.

Anders Søgaard. 2008. Range concatenation grammars for translation. In *Proceedings of the 22nd International Conference on Computational Linguistics, Companion Volume*, pages 103–106, Manchester, England.

Raghavendra Udupa and Hemanta Maji. 2006. Computational complexity of statistical machine translation. In *Proceedings of the 11th Conference of the European Chapter of the Association for Computational Linguistics*, pages 25–32, Trento, Italy.

Dekai Wu. 1997. Stochastic inversion transduction grammars and bilingual parsing of parallel corpora. *Computational Linguistics*, 23(3):377–403.

Hao Zhang and Daniel Gildea. 2004. Syntax-based alignment: supervised or unsupervised? In *Proceedings of the 20th International Conference on Computational Linguistics*, pages 418–424, Geneva, Switzerland.

Reordering Model Using Syntactic Information of a Source Tree for Statistical Machine Translation

Kei Hashimoto[*1], **Hirohumi Yamamoto**[*2*3], **Hideo Okuma**[*2*4],
Eiichiro Sumita[*2*4], **and Keiichi Tokuda**[*1*2]
[*1]Nagoya Institute of Technology Department of Computer Science and Engineering
/ Gokiso-cho Syouwa-ku Nagoya-city Aichi Japan
[*2]National Institute of Information and Communications Technology
[*3]Kinki University School of Science and Engineering Department of Informaiton
[*4]ATR Spoken Language Communication Research Labs.

Abstract

This paper presents a reordering model using syntactic information of a source tree for phrase-based statistical machine translation. The proposed model is an extension of IST-ITG (imposing source tree on inversion transduction grammar) constraints. In the proposed method, the target-side word order is obtained by rotating nodes of the source-side parse-tree. We modeled the node rotation, monotone or swap, using word alignments based on a training parallel corpus and source-side parse-trees. The model efficiently suppresses erroneous target word orderings, especially global orderings. Furthermore, the proposed method conducts a probabilistic evaluation of target word reorderings. In English-to-Japanese and English-to-Chinese translation experiments, the proposed method resulted in a 0.49-point improvement (29.31 to 29.80) and a 0.33-point improvement (18.60 to 18.93) in word BLEU-4 compared with IST-ITG constraints, respectively. This indicates the validity of the proposed reordering model.

1 Introduction

Statistical machine translation has been wiedely applied in many state-of-the-art translation systems. A popular statistical machine translation paradigms is the phrase-based model (Koehn et al., 2003; Och and Ney, 2004). In phrase-based statistical machine translation, errors in word reordering, especially global reordering, are one of the most serious problems. To resolve this problem, many word-reordering constraint techniques have been proposed. These techniques are categorized into two types. The first type is linguistically syntax-based. In this approach, tree structures for the source (Quirk et al., 2005; Huang et al., 2006), target (Yamada and Knight, 2000; Marcu et al., 2006), or both (Melamed, 2004) are used for model training. The second type is formal constraints on word permutations. IBM constraints (Berger et al., 1996), the lexical word reordering model (Tillmann, 2004), and inversion transduction grammar (ITG) constraints (Wu, 1995; Wu, 1997) belong to this type of approach. For ITG constraints, the target-side word order is obtained by rotating nodes of the source-side binary tree. In these node rotations, the source binary tree instance is not considered. Imposing a source tree on ITG (IST-ITG) constraints (Yamamoto et al., 2008) is an extension of ITG constraints and a hybrid of the first and second type of approach. IST-ITG constraints directly introduce a source sentence tree structure. Therefore, IST-ITG can obtain stronger constraints for word reordering than the original ITG constraints. For example, IST-ITG constraints allows only eight word orderings for a four-word sentence, even though twenty-two word orderings are possible with respect to the original ITG constraints. Although IST-ITG constraints efficiently suppress erroneous target word orderings, the method cannot assign the probability to the target word orderings.

This paper presents a reordering model using syntactic information of a source tree for phrase-based statistical machine translation. The proposed reordering model is an extension of IST-ITG con-

Proceedings of SSST-3, Third Workshop on Syntax and Structure in Statistical Translation, pages 69–77,
Boulder, Colorado, June 2009.

straints. In the proposed method, the target-side word order is obtained by rotating nodes of a source-side parse-tree in a similar fashion to IST-ITG constraints. We modeled the rotating positions, monotone or swap, from word alignments of a training parallel corpus and source-side parse-trees. The proposed method conducts a probabilistic evaluation of target word orderings using syntactic information of the source tree.

The rest of this paper is organized as follows. Section 2 describes the previous approach to resolving erroneous word reordering. In Section 3, the reordering model using syntactic information of a source tree is presented. Section 4 shows experimental results. Finally, Section 5 presnts the summary and some concluding remarks and future works.

2 Previous Works

First, we introduce two previous studies on related word reordering constraints, ITG and IST-ITG constraints.

2.1 ITG Constraints

In one-to-one word-alignment, the source word f_i is translated into the target word e_i. The source sentence $[f_1, f_2, \cdots, f_N]$ is translated into the target sentence which is the reordered target word sequence $[e_1, e_2, \cdots, e_N]$. The number of reorderings is $N!$. When ITG constraints are introduced, this combination $N!$ can be reduced in accordance with the following constraints.

- All possible binary tree structures are generated from the source word sequence.
- The target sentence is obtained by rotating any node of the binary trees.

When $N = 4$, the ITG constraints can reduce the number of combinations from $4! = 24$ to 22 by rejecting the combinations $[e_3, e_1, e_4, e_2]$ and $[e_2, e_4, e_1, e_3]$. For a four-word sentence, the search space is reduced to 92% (22/24), but for a 10-word sentence, the search space is only 6% (206,098/3,628,800) of the original full space.

2.2 IST-ITG Constraints

In ITG constraints, the source-side binary tree instance is not considered. Therefore, if a source sentence tree structure is utilized, stronger constraints than the original ITG constraints can be created. IST-ITG constraints directly introduce a source sentence tree structure. The target sentence is obtained with the following constraints.

- A source sentence tree structure is generated from the source sentence.
- The target sentence is obtained by rotating any node of the source sentence tree structure.

By parsing the source sentence, the parse-tree is obtained. After parsing the source sentence, a bracketed sentence is obtained by removing the node syntactic labels; this bracketed sentence can then be converted into a tree structure. For example, the parse-tree "(S1 (S (NP (DT This)) (VP (AUX is) (NP (DT a) (NN pen)))))" is obtained from the source sentence "This is a pen," which consists of four words. By removing the node syntactic labels, the bracketed sentence "((This) ((is) ((a) (pen))))" is obtained. Such a bracketed sentence can be used to produce constraints. If IST-ITG constraints is applied, the number of word orderings in $N = 4$ is reduced to 8, down from 22 with ITG cnstraints. For example, for the source-side bracketed tree "$((f_1 f_2)\ (f_3 f_4))$," the eight target sequences $[e_1, e_2, e_3, e_4]$, $[e_2, e_1, e_3, e_4]$, $[e_1, e_2, e_4, e_3]$, $[e_2, e_1, e_4, e_3]$, $[e_3, e_4, e_1, e_2]$, $[e_3, e_4, e_2, e_1]$, $[e_4, e_3, e_1, e_2]$, and $[e_4, e_3, e_2, e_1]$ are accepted. For the source-side bracketed tree "$(((f_1 f_2)\ f_3)\ f_4)$," the eight sequences $[e_1, e_2, e_3, e_4]$, $[e_2, e_1, e_3, e_4]$, $[e_3, e_1, e_2, e_4]$, $[e_3, e_2, e_1, e_4]$, $[e_4, e_1, e_2, e_3]$, $[e_4, e_2, e_1, e_3]$, $[e_4, e_3, e_1, e_2]$, and $[e_4, e_3, e_2, e_1]$ are accepted. When the source sentence tree structure is a binary tree, the number of word orderings is reduced to 2^{N-1}. The parsing results sometimes do not produce binary trees. In this case, some subtrees have more than two child nodes. For a non-binary subtree, any reordering of child nodes is allowed. If a subtree has three child nodes, six reorderings of the nodes are accepted.

In phrase-based statistical machine translation, a source "phrase" is translated into a target "phrase". However, with IST-ITG constraints, "word" must be used for the constraint unit since the parse unit is a "word". To absorb different units between translation models and IST-ITG constraints, a new limitation for word reordering is applied.

- Word ordering that destroys a phrase is not allowed.

When this limitation is applied, the translated word ordering is obtained from the bracketed source sentence tree by reordering the nodes in the tree, which is the same as for one-to-one word-alignment.

3 Reordering Model Using Syntactic Information of the Source Tree

In this section, we present a new reordering model using syntactic information of a source-side parse-tree.

3.1 Abstract of Proposed Method

The IST-ITG constraints method efficiently suppresses erroneous target word orderings. However, IST-ITG constraints cannot evaluate the accuracy of the target word orderings; i.e., IST-ITG constraints assign an equal probability to all target word orderings. This paper proposes a reordering model using syntactic information of the source tree as an extension of IST-ITG constraints. The proposed reordering model conducts a probabilistic evaluation of target word orderings using syntactic information of the source-side parse-tree.

In the proposed method, the target-side word order is obtained by rotating nodes of the source-side parse-tree in a similar fashion to IST-ITG constraints. Reordering probabilities are assigned to each subtree of source-side parse-tree S by reordering the positions into two types: monotone and swap. If the subtree has more than two child nodes, the number of child node order is more than two. However, we assume the child node order other than monotone to be swap. The source-side parse-tree S consists of subtrees $\{s_1, s_2, \cdots, s_K\}$, where K is the number of subtrees included in the source-side parse-tree. The subtree s_k is which is represented by the parent node's syntactic label and the order, from sentence head to sentence tail, of the child node's syntactic labels. For example, Figure 1 shows a source-side parse-tree for a four-word

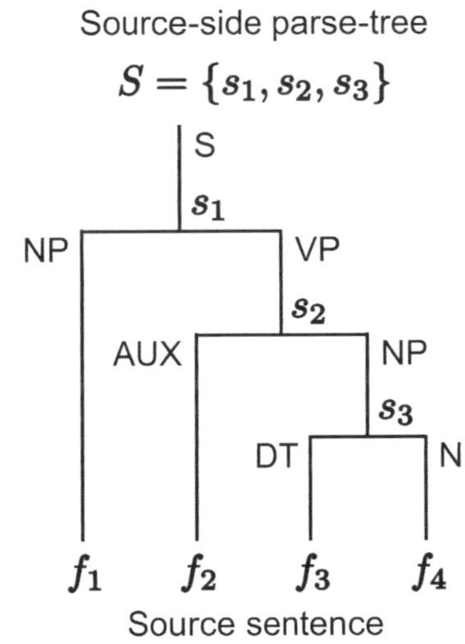

Figure 1: Example of a source-side parse-tree fo a four-word source sentence consisting of three subtrees.

source sentence consisting of three subtrees. In Figure 1, the subtrees s_1, s_2, and s_3 are represented by **S+NP+VP**, **VP+AUX+NP**, and **NP+DT+NN**, respectively. Each subtree has a probability $P(t \mid s_k)$, where t is monotone (m) or swap (s). The probability of the target word reordering is calculated as follows.

$$P_r = \prod_{k=1}^{K} P(t \mid s_k) \qquad (1)$$

Each target candidate is assigned the different reordering probability by Equation (1). Since the proposed reordering model uses the syntactic labels, which is not considered in IST-ITG constraints, the different parse-tree assigns the different reordering probability. The proposed model is effective for global word reordering, because reordering probabilities are also assigned to higher-level subtrees of the source-side parse-tree.

3.2 Training of the Proposed Model

We modeled monotone or swap node rotating automatically from word alignments of a training parallel corpus and source-side parse-trees. The training algorithm for the proposed reordering model is as follows.

1. The training process begins with a word-aligned corpus. We obtained the word alignments using Koehn et al.'s method (2003),

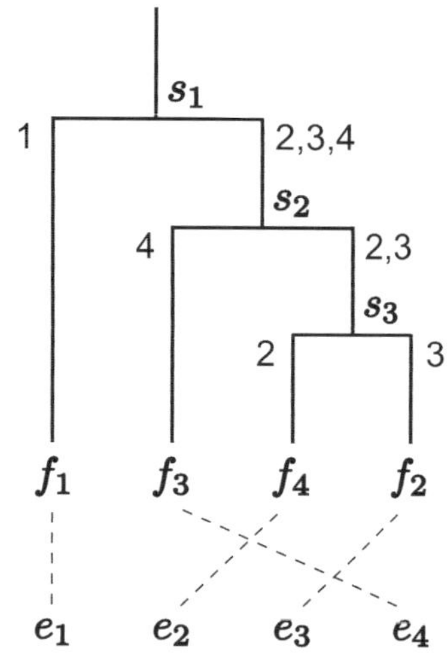

Figure 2: Example of a source-side parse-tree with word alignments using the training algorithm of the proposed model.

which is based on Och and Ney's work (2004). This involves running GIZA++ (Och and Ney, 2003) on the corpus in both directions, and applying refinement rules (the variant they designate is "final-and") to obtain a single many-to-many word alignment for each sentence.

2. Source-side parse-trees are created using a source language phrase structure parser, which annotates each node with a syntactic label. A source-side parse-tree consists of several subtrees with syntactic labels. For example, the parse-tree "(S1 (S (NP (DT This)) (VP (AUX is) (NP (DT a) (NN pen)))))" is obtained from the source sentence "This is a pen" which consists of four words.

3. Word alignments and source-side parse-trees are combined. Leaf nodes are assigned target word positions obtained from word alignments. Via the bottom-up process, target word positions are assigned to all nodes. For example, in Figure 2, the left-side (sentence head) child node of subtree s_2 is assigned the target word position "4," and the right-side (sentence tail) child node is assigned the target word positions "2" and "3," which are assigned to the child nodes of subtree s_3.

4. The monotone and swap reordering positions are checked and counted for each subtree. By comparing the target word positions, which are assigned in the above step, the reordering position is determined. If the target word position of the left-side child node is smaller than one of the right-side child node, the reordering position determined as monotone. For example, in Figure 2, the subtrees s_1, s_2 and s_3 are monotone, swap, and monotone, respectively.

Subtree type	Monotone probability
S+PP+,+NP+VP+.	0.764
PP+IN+NP	0.816
NP+DT+NN+NN	0.664
VP+AUX+VP	0.864
VP+VBN+PP	0.837
NP+NP+PP	0.805
NP+DT+JJ+NN	0.653
NP+DT+JJ+VBP+NN	0.412
NP+DT+NN+CC+VB	0.357

Table 1: Example of proposed reordering models.

5. The reordering probability of the subtree can be directly estimated by counting the reordering positions in the training data.

$$P(t \mid s) = \frac{c_t(s)}{\sum_t c_t(s)} \qquad (2)$$

where $c_t(s)$ is the count of reordering positon t included all training samples for the subtree s.

The parsing results sometimes do not produce binary trees. For a non-binary subtree, any reordering of child nodes is allowed. However, the proposed reordering model assumes that reordering positions are only two, monotone and swap. That is, the reordering position which the order of child nodes do not change is monotone, and the other positions are swap. Therefore, the probability of swap $P(\mathrm{s} \mid s_k)$ is derived from the probability of monotone $P(\mathrm{m} \mid s_k)$ as follows.

$$P(\mathrm{s} \mid s_k) = 1.0 - P(\mathrm{m} \mid s_k) \qquad (3)$$

Table 1 shows the example of proposed reordering models.

If a subtree is represented by a binary-tree, there are L^3 possible subtrees, where L is the number of

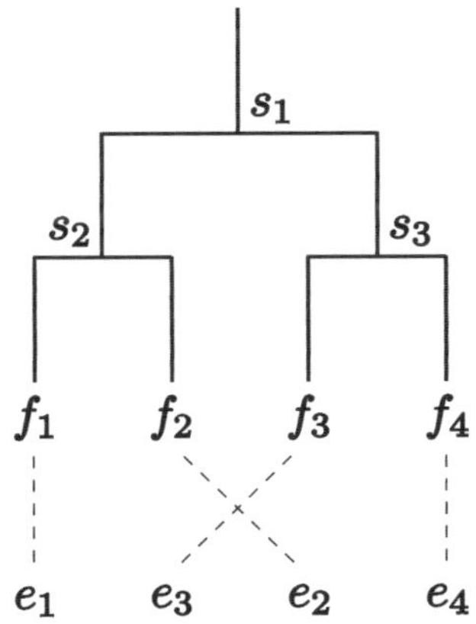

Figure 3: Example of a target word order which is not derived from rotating the nodes of source-side parse trees.

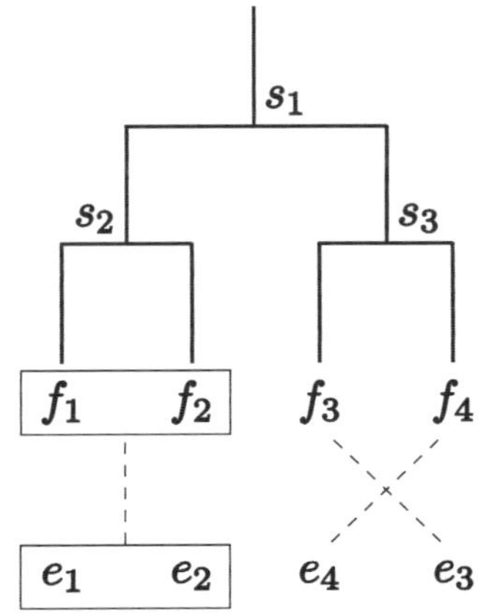

Figure 4: Example of a target candidate including a phrase.

syntactic labels. However, in the possible subtrees, there are subtrees observed only a few times in training sentences, especially when the subtree consists of more than three child nodes. Although a large number of subtree models can capture variations in the training samples, too many models lead to the over-fitting problem. Therefore, subtrees where the number of training samples is less than a heuristic threshold and unseen subtrees are clustered to deal with the data sparseness problem for robust model estimations.

After creating word alignments of a training parallel corpus, there are target word orders which are not derived from rotating nodes of source-side parse-trees. Figure 3 shows a sample which is not derived from rotating nodes. Some are due to linguistic reasons, structual differences such as negation (French "ne...pas" and English "not"), adverb, modal and so on. Others are due to non-linguistic reasons, errors of automatic word alignments, syntactic analysis, or human translation (Fox, 2002). The proposed method discards such problematic cases. In Figure 3, the subtree s_1 is then removed from training samples, and the subtrees s_2 and s_3 are used as training samples.

3.3 Decoding Using the Proposed Reordering Model

In this section, we describe a one-pass phrase-based decoding algorithm that uses the proposed reordering model in the decoder. The translation target sentence is sequentially generated from left (sentence head) to right (sentence tail), and all reordering is conducted on the source side. To introduce the proposed reordering model into the decoder, the target candidate must be checked for whether the reordering position of a subtree is either monotone or swap whenever a new phrase is selected to extend a target candidate. The checking algorithm is as follows.

1. For old translation candidates, the subtree s, which includes both translated and untranslated words, and its untranslated part u are calculated.
2. When a new target phrase $\bar{e}$ is generated, the source phrase $\bar{f}$ and the untranslated part u calculated in the above step are compared. If the source phrase $\bar{f}$ does not include the untranslated part u and is not included u, the new candidate is rejected.
3. In the accepted candidate, the reordering positions for all subtrees included the source side parse-tree are checked by comparing the source phrase $\bar{f}$ with the source phrase sequence used before.

Subtrees checked reordering positions are assigned a probability–monotone or swap–by the proposed reordering model, and the target word order is evaluated by Equation (1).

Phrase-based statistical machine translation uses a "phrase" as the translation unit. However, the proposed reordering model needs a "word" order. Because "word" alignments form the source phrase to target phrase are not clear, we cannot determine the

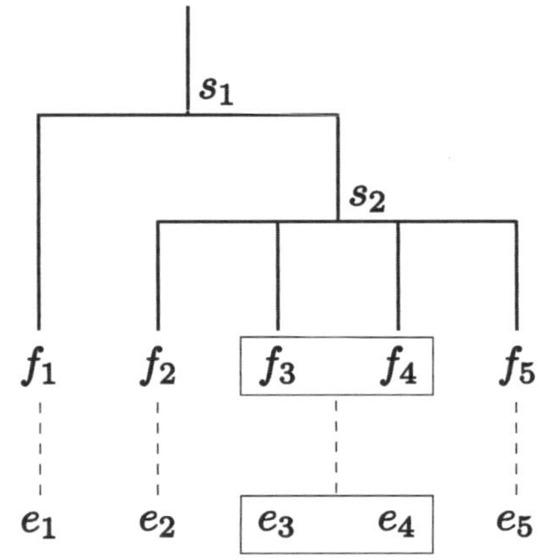

Figure 5: Example of a non-binary subtree including a phrase.

reordering position of subtree included in a phrase. Therefore, in the decoding process using the proposed reordering model, we define that higher probability, monotone or swap, are assigned to subtrees included in a source phrase. For example, in Figure 4, the source sentence $[[f_1, f_2], f_3, f_4]$ is translated into the target sentence $[[e_1, e_2], e_4, e_3]$, where $[f_1, f_2]$ and $[e_1, e_2]$ are used as phrases. Then, the source phrase $[f_1, f_2]$ includes the subtree s_2. If the monotone probabilities of subtrees s_1, s_2, and s_3 are 0.8, 0.4 and 0.7, the proposed reordering probability is $0.8 \times 0.6 \times 0.3 = 0.144$. If a source phrase is $[f_1, f_2, f_3, f_4]$ and a source-side parse-tree has the same tree structure used in Figure 4, the subtrees s_1, s_2, and s_3 are assigned higher reordering probabilities. If the source phrase $[f_1, f_2, f_3, f_4]$ used in Figure 4, the subtrees s_1, s_2, and s_3 are assigned higher reordering probabilities.

Non-binary subtrees are often observed in the source-side parse-tree. When a source phrase $\bar{f}$ is included in a non-binary subtree and does not include a non-binary subtree, we cannot determine the reordering position. For example, the reordering position of subtree s_2 in Figure 5, which includes the phrase $[f_3, f_4]$, can not be determined. In this case, we define that such subtrees are also to be assigned a higher probability.

4 Experiments

To evaluate the proposed model, we conducted two experiments: English-to-Japanese and English-to-Chinese translation.

		English	Japanese
Train	Sentences	1.0M	
	Words	24.6M	24.6M
Dev	Sentences	2.0K	
	Words	50.1K	58.7K
Test	Sentences	2.0K	
	Words	49.5K	58.0K

Table 2: Statistics of training, development and test corpus for E-J translation.

4.1 English-to-Japanese Paper Abstract Translation Experiments

The first experiment was the English-to-Japanese (E-J) translation. Table 2 shows the training, development and test corpus statistics. JST Japanese-English paper abstract corpus consists of 1.0M parallel sentences were used for model training. This corpus was constructed from 2.0M Japanese-English paper abstract corpus belongs to JST by NICT using the method of Uchiyama and Isahara (2007). For phrase-based translation model training, we used the GIZA++ toolkit (Och and Ney, 2003), and 1.0M bilingual sentences. For language model training, we used the SRI language model toolkit (Stolcke, 2002), and 1.0M sentences for the translation model training. The language model type was word 5-gram smoothed by Kneser-Ney discounting (Kneser and Ney, 1995). To tune the decoder parameters, we conducted minimum error rate training (Och, 2003) with respect to the word BLEU score (Papineni et al., 2002) using 2.0K development sentence pairs. The test set with 2.0K sentences is used. In the evaluation and development sets, a single reference was used. For the creation of English sentence parse trees and segmentation of the English, we used the Charniak parser (Charniak, 2000). We used Chasen for segmentation of the Japanese sentences. For decoding, we used an in-house decoder that is a close relative of the Moses decoder. The performance of this decoder was configured to be the same as Moses. Other conditions were the same as the default conditions of the Moses decoder.

In this experiment, the following three methods were compared.

- Baseline : The IBM constraints and the lexical reordering model were used for target word

	Baseline	IST-ITG	Proposed
BLEU	27.87	29.31	29.80

Table 3: BLEU score results for E-J translation. (1-reference)

reordering.

- IST-ITG : The IST-ITG constraints, the IBM constraints, and the lexical reordering model were used for target word reordering.

- Proposed : The proposed reordering model, the IBM constraints, and the lexical reordering model were used for target word reordering.

During minimum error training, each method used each reordering model and reordering constraint.

The proposed reordering model are trained from 1.0M bilingual sentences for the translation model training. The amount of available training samples represented by subtrees was 9.8M. In the available training samples, there were 54K subtree types. The heuristic threshold was 10, and subtrees with training samples of less than 10 were clustered. The proposed reordering model consisted of 5,960 subtrees types and one clustered model "other". The models not including "other" covered 99.29% of all training samples.

The BLEU scores are presented in Table 3. In comparing "Baseline" method with "IST-ITG" method, the improvement in BLEU was a 1.44-point. Furthermore, in comparing "IST-ITG" method with "Proposed" method, the improvement in BLEU was a 0.49-point. Both the IST-ITG constraints and the proposed reordering model fixed the phrase position for the global reorderings. However, the proposed method can conduct a probabilistic evaluation of target word reorderings which the IST-ITG constraints cannot. Therefore, "Proposed" method resulted in a better BLEU.

4.2 NIST MT08 English-to-Chinese Translation Experiments

Next, we conducted English-to-Chinese (E-C) newspaper translation experiments for different language pairs. The NIST MT08 evaluation campaign English-to-Chinese translation track was used for the training and evaluation corpora. Table 4 shows the training, development and test corpus statistics. For the translation model training, we used 4.6M bilingual sentences. For the language model training, we used 4.6M sentences which are used for the translation model training. The language model type was word 3-gram smoothed by Kneser-Ney discounting. A development set with 1.6K sentences was used as evaluation data in the Chinese-to-English translation track for the NIST MT07 evaluation campaign. A single reference was used in the development set. The evaluation set with 1.9K sentences is the same as the MT08 evaluation data, with 4 references. In this experiment, the compared methods were the same as in the E-J experiment.

		English	Chinese
Train	Sentences	4.6M	
	Words	79.6M	73.4M
Dev	Sentences	1.6K	
	Words	46.4K	39.0K
Test	Sentences	1.9K	
	Words	45.7K	47.0K (Ave.)

Table 4: Statistics of training, development and test corpus for E-C translation.

	Baseline	IST-ITG	Proposed
BLEU	17.54	18.60	18.93

Table 5: BLEU score results for E-C translation. (4-reference)

The proposed reordering model are trained from 4.6M bilingual sentences for the translation model training. The amount of available training samples represented by subtrees was 39.6M. In the available training samples, there were 193K subtree types. As in the E-J experiments, the heuristic threshold was 10. The proposed reordering model consisted of 18,955 subtree types and one clustered model "other." The models not including "other" covered 99.45% of all training samples.

The BLEU scores are presented in Table 5. In comparing "Baseline" method with "IST-ITG" method, the improvement in BLEU was a 1.06-point. In comparing "IST-ITG" method with "Proposed" method, the improvement in BLEU was a 0.33-point. As in the E-J experiments, "Proposed" method performed the highest BLEU. We demonstrated that the proposed method is effective for multiple language pairs. However, the improvement of BLEU score in E-C translation is smaller than the improvement in E-J translation, because English and Chinese are similar sentence structures, such as SVO-languages (Japanese is SOV-language). When the sentence structures are different, the proposed reordering model is effective.

5 Conclusion

This paper proposed a new word reordering model using syntactic information of a source tree for phrase-based statistical machine translation. The proposed model is an extension of the IST-ITG constraints. In both IST-ITG constraints and the proposed method, the target-side word order is obtained by rotating nodes of the source-side tree structure. Both the IST-ITG constraints and the proposed reordering model fix the phrase position for the global reorderings. However, the proposed method can conduct a probabilistic evaluation of target word reorderings which the IST-ITG constraints cannot. In E-J and E-C translation experiments, the proposed method resulted in a 0.49-point improvement (29.31 to 29.80) and a 0.33-point improvement (18.60 to 18.93) in word BLEU-4 compared with IST-ITG constraints, respectively. This indicates the validity of the proposed reordering model.

Future work will focus on a reduction of computational cost of decoding including the proposed reordering model, and a simultaneous training of translation and reordering models. Moreover, we will deal with difference between source and target in multi level like in Gally et al. (2004).

The improvement could clearly be seen from visual inspection of the output, a few examples of which are presented in the following Appendix.

A Samples from the English-to-Japanese Translation

A.1 Sentence 1

Source: Aggravation was obvious from the latter half of March to the end of April, and he contracted the disease in February to the beginning of May.
Baseline: ４月末に３月後半から５月上旬に２月に疾患を発症し，著明な増悪した。
Reference: ３月後半から４月末に増悪が著明で，２～５月上旬に発症した。
Proposed: ３月後半から４月末に著明な増悪し，５月上旬に２月に疾患を発症した。

A.2 Sentence 2

Source: The value of TF, on the other hand, was higher in the reverse order, indicating that high oxidation rate causes severe defects on the surface of Ni crystallites.
Baseline: 一方，重症の表面上の欠陥の原因となることを示し，逆順に高かったが，ＴＦの値は高い酸化速度はＮｉの微結晶た。
Reference: 一方，ＴＦの値は逆の順序で高く，酸化速度が高いことはＮｉ結晶の表面欠陥の原因になることを示した。
Proposed: 一方，ＴＦの値は逆の順序で高かったことを示し，高い酸化速度は，Ｎｉの微結晶表面に重篤な欠陥の原因となる。

A.3 Sentence 3

Source: After diagnosing the pleural effusion and ascites, vein catheter was left in place under the echo guide, and after removing the pleural effusion and ascites, OK-432 was administered locally.
Baseline: 診断後，胸水，腹水，胸水・腹水を除去した後，エコーガイド下で，静脈カテーテルを左に代わってＯＫ－　４３２を投与した。
Reference: 胸水・腹水の診断を行った後にエコーガイド下に静脈カテーテルを留置し，胸水・腹水を除去し，ＯＫ－　４３２を局所投与した。
Proposed: 胸水・腹水の診断後，静脈カテーテルを残したエコーガイド下で代わりに，胸水・腹水を除去した後，ＯＫ－　４３２，局所的に投与した。

A.4 Sentence 4

Source: From result of the consideration, it was pointed that radiation from the loop elements was weak.
Baseline: 考察の結果からことを指摘し，ループ素子からの放射は弱かった。
Reference: 考察結果より，ループ素子からの放射が弱いことを指摘する。
Proposed: 考察の結果から，ループ素子からの放射は弱いことを示した。

References

Adam L. Berger, Peter F. Brown, Stephen A. Della Pietra, Vincent J. Della Pietra, Andrew S. Kehler, and Robert L. Mercer 1996. Language translation apparatus and method of using context-based translation models. United States patent, patent number 5510981.

Eugene Charniak. 2000. A Maximum-Entropy-Inspired Parser. In *Proceedings of NAACL 2000*, pages 132–139.

Chasen
http://chasen-legacy.sourceforge.jp/

Heidi J. Fox, 2002. Phrasal cohesion and statistical machine translation. In *Proceedings of EMNLP*, pages 304–311.

Michel Galley, Mark Hopkins, Kevin Knight, and Daniel Marcu. 2004. What's in a translation rule? In *Proceedings of HLT/NAACL-04*.

Liang Huang, Kevin Knight, and Aravind Joshi. 2006. Statistical Syntax-Directed Translation with Extended Domain of Locality. In *Proceedings of AMTA*.

Japanese-English paper abstract corpus
http://www.jst.go.jp

Reinhard Kneser and Hermann Ney. 1995. Improved backing-off for m-gram language model In *Proceedings of ICASSP 1995*, pages 181–184.

Philipp Koehn, Franz Josef Och, and Daniel Marcu. 2003. Statistical phrase-based translation. In *Proceedings of HLT-NAACL 2003*, pages 127–133.

Daniel Marcu, Wei Wang, Abdessamad Echihabi, and Kevin Knight. 2006. SPMT: Statistical Machine Translation with Syntactified Target Language Phrases In *Proceedings of EMNLP2006*, pages 44–52.

Dan Melamed. 2004. Statistical machine translation by parsing In *Proceedings of ACL*, pages 653–660.

Moses
http://www.statmt.org/moses/

Franz josef Och and Hermann Ney. 2003. A Systematic Comparison of Various Statistical Alignment Models. *Computational Linguistics*, 29(1), pages 19–51.

Franz josef Och. 2003. Minimum error rate training for statistical machine translation. In *Proceedings of ACL*, pages 160–167.

Franz josef Och and Hermann Ney. 2004. The alignment template approach to statistical machine translation. *Computational Linguistics*, 30(4), pages 417–449.

Chris Quirk, Arul Menezes, and Colin Cherry. 2005. Dependency treelet translation: Syntactically informed phrasal SMT. In *Proceedings of ACL*, pages 271–279.

Kishore Papineni, Salim Roukos, Todd Ward, and Wei-Jing Zhu. 2002. Bleu: a method for automatic evaluation of machine translation. In *Proceedings of ACL*, pages 311–318.

Andreas Stolcke. 2002. SRILM - An Extensible Language Model Toolkit In *Proceedings of ICSLP2002*, pages 901–904. http://www.speech.sri.com/projects/srilm/

Christopher Tillmann. 2004. A unigram orientation model for statistical machine translation. In *Proceedings of HLT-NAACL*, pages 101–104.

Masao Uchiyama and Hitoshi Isahara. 2007. 2007. A japanese-english patent parallel corpus. In MT summit XI, pages 475–482.

Dekai Wu. 1995. Stochastic inversion transduction grammars, with application to segmentation, bracketing, and alignment of parallel corpora. In *Proceedings of IJCAI*, pages 1328–1334.

Dekai Wu. 1997. Stochastic inversion transduction grammars and bilingual parsing of parallel corpora. *Computational Linguiatics*, 23(3), pages 377–403.

Kenji Yamada and Kevin Knight. 2000. A syntax-based statistical translation model In *Proceedings of ACL*, pages 523–530.

Hirofumi Yamamoto, Hideo Okuma, and Eiichiro Sumita. 2008. Imposing Constraints from the Source Tree on ITG Constraints for SMT. In *Proceedings of ACL : HLT Second Workshop on Syntax and Structure in Statistical Translation (SSST-2)*, pages 1–9.

Coupling hierarchical word reordering and decoding in phrase-based statistical machine translation

Maxim Khalilov and **José A.R. Fonollosa**
Universitat Politècnica de Catalunya
Campus Nord UPC, 08034,
Barcelona, Spain
{khalilov,adrian}@gps.tsc.upc.edu

Mark Dras
Macquarie University
North Ryde NSW 2109,
Sydney, Australia
madras@ics.mq.edu.au

Abstract

In this paper, we start with the existing idea of taking reordering rules automatically derived from syntactic representations, and applying them in a preprocessing step before translation to make the source sentence structurally more like the target; and we propose a new approach to hierarchically extracting these rules. We evaluate this, combined with a lattice-based decoding, and show improvements over state-of-the-art distortion models.

1 Introduction

One of the big challenges for the MT community is the problem of placing translated words in a natural order. This issue originates from the fact that different languages are characterized by different word order requirements. The problem is especially important if the distance between words which should be reordered is high (global reordering); in this case the reordering decision is very difficult to take based on statistical information due to dramatic expansion of the search space with the increase in number of words involved in the search process.

Classically, statistical machine translation (SMT) systems do not incorporate any linguistic analysis and work at the surface level of word forms. However, more recently MT systems are moving towards including additional linguistic and syntactic informative sources (for example, source- and/or target-side syntax) into word reordering process. In this paper we propose using a syntactic reordering system operating with fully, partially and non- lexicalized reordering patterns, which are applied on the step prior to translation; the novel idea in this paper is in the derivation of these rules in a hierarchical manner, inspired by Imamura et al (2005). Furthermore, we propose generating a word lattice from the bilingual corpus with the reordered source side, extending the search space on the decoding step. A thorough study of the combination of syntactical and word lattice reordering approaches is another novelty of the paper.

2 Related work

Many reordering algorithms have appeared over the past few years. Word class-based reordering was a part of Och's Alignment Template system (Och et al., 2004); the main criticism of this approach is that it shows bad performance for the pair of languages with very distinct word order. The state-of-the-art SMT system Moses implements a distance-based reordering model (Koehn et al., 2003) and a distortion model, operating with rewrite patterns extracted from a phrase alignment table (Tillman, 2004).

Many SMT models implement the brute force approach, introducing several constrains for the reordering search as described in Kanthak et al. (2005) and Crego et al. (2005). The main criticism of such systems is that the constraints are not lexicalized. Recently there has been interest in SMT exploiting non-monotonic decoding which allow for extension of the search space and linguistic information involvement. The variety of such models includes a constrained distance-based reordering (Costa-jussà et al., 2006); and a constrained version of distortion model where the reordering search problem is tackled through a set of linguistically motivated rules used during decoding (Crego and Mariño, 2007).

Proceedings of SSST-3, Third Workshop on Syntax and Structure in Statistical Translation, pages 78–86,
Boulder, Colorado, June 2009.

A quite popular class of reordering algorithms is a monotonization of the source part of the parallel corpus prior to translation. The first work on this approach is described in Nießen and Ney (2004), where morpho-syntactic information was used to account for the reorderings needed. A representative set of similar systems includes: a set of hand-crafted reordering patterns for German-to-English (Collins et al., 2005) and Chinese-English (Wang et al., 2007) translations, emphasizing the distinction between German/Chinese and English clause structure; and statistical machine reordering (SMR) technique where a monotonization of the source words sequence is performed by translating them into the reordered one using well established SMT mechanism (Costa-jussà and Fonollosa, 2006). Coupling of SMR algorithm and the search space extension via generating a set of weighted reordering hypotheses has demonstrated a significant improvement, as shown in Costa-jussà and Fonollosa (2008).

The technique proposed in this study is most similar to the one proposed for French-to-English translation task in Xia and McCord (2004), where the authors present a hybrid system for French-English translation based on the principle of automatic rewrite patterns extraction using a parse tree and phrase alignments. We propose using a word distortion model not only to monotonize the source part of the corpus (using a different approach to rewrite rule organization from Xia and McCord), but also to extend the search space during decoding.

3 Baseline phrase-based SMT systems

The reference system which was used as a translation mechanism is the state-of-the-art Moses-based SMT (Koehn et al., 2007). The training and weights tuning procedures can be found on the Moses web page[1].

Classical phrase-based translation is considered as a three step algorithm: (1) the source sequence of words is segmented into phrases, (2) each phrase is translated into the target language using a translation table, (3) the target phrases are reordered to fit the target language. The probabilities of the phrases are estimated by relative frequencies of their appearance in the training corpus.

[1] http://www.statmt.org/moses/

In baseline experiments we used a phrase dependent lexicalized reordering model, as proposed in Tillmann (2004). According to this model, monotonic or reordered local orientations enriched with probabilities are learned from training data. During decoding, translation is viewed as a monotone block sequence generation process with the possibility to swap a pair of neighbor blocks.

4 Syntax-based reordering coupled with word graph

Our syntax-based reordering system requires access to source and target language parse trees and word alignments intersections.

4.1 Notation

Syntax-based reordering (SBR) operates with source and target parse trees that represent the syntactic structure of a string in source and target languages according to a Context-Free Grammar (CFG).

We call this representation *"CFG form"*. We formally define a CFG in the usual way as $G = \langle N, T, R, S \rangle$, where N is a set of nonterminal symbols (corresponding to source-side phrase and part-of-speech tags); T is a set of source-side terminals (the lexicon), R is a set of production rules of the form $\eta \rightarrow \gamma$, with $\eta \in N$ and γ, which is a sequence of terminal and nonterminal symbols; and $S \in N$ is the distinguished symbol.

The reordering rules then have the form

$$\eta_0 @0 \ldots \eta_k @k \rightarrow \eta_{d_0} @d_0 \ldots \eta_{d_k} @d_k | Lexicon | p_1 \quad (1)$$

where $\eta_i \in N$ for all $0 \leq i \leq k$; $(d_o \ldots d_k)$ is a permutation of $(0 \ldots k)$; *Lexicon* comes from the source-side set of words for each η_i; and p_1 is a probability associated with the rule. Figure 1 gives two examples of the rule format.

4.2 Rules extraction

Concept. Inspired by the ideas presented in Imamura et al. (2005), where monolingual correspondences of syntactic nodes are used during decoding, we extract a set of bilingual patterns allowing for reordering as described below:

(1) align the monotone bilingual corpus with GIZA++ (Och and Ney, 2003) and find the intersection of direct and inverse word alignments, resulting in the construction of the projection matrix P (see below));

(2) parse the source and the target parts of the parallel corpus;

(3) extract reordering patterns from the parallel non-isomorphic CFG-trees based on the word alignment intersection.

Step 2 is straightforward; we explain aspects of Steps 1 and 3 in more detail below. Figures 1 and 2 show an example of the extraction of two lexicalized rules for a parallel Arabic-English sentence:

Arabic: *h*A hW fndq +k*
English: this is your hotel

We use this below in our explanations.

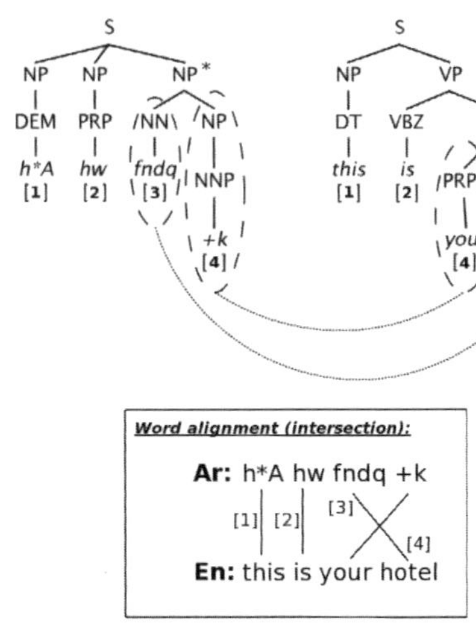

Figure 2: Example of subtree transfer and reordering rules extraction.

Projection matrix. Bilingual content can be represented in the form of words or sequences of words depending on the syntactic role of the corresponding grammatical element (constituent or POS).

Given two parse trees and a word alignment intersection, a projection matrix P is defined as an $M \times N$ matrix such that M is the number of words in the target phrase; N is the number of words in the source phrase; and a cell (i, j) has a value based on the alignment intersection — this value is zero if word i and word j do not align, and is a unique non-zero link number if they do.

For the trees in Figure 2,

$$P = \begin{pmatrix} 1 & 0 & 0 & 0 \\ 0 & 2 & 0 & 0 \\ 0 & 0 & 0 & 3 \\ 0 & 0 & 4 & 0 \end{pmatrix}$$

Unary chains. Given an unary chain of the form $X \rightarrow Y$, rules are extracted for each level in this chain. For example given a rule

$$NP@0\, ADVP@1 \rightarrow ADVP@1\, NP@0$$

and a unary chain "$ADVP \rightarrow AD$", a following equivalent rule will be generated

$$NP@0\, AD@1 \rightarrow AD@1\, NP@0.$$

The role of target-side parse tree. Although reordering is performed on the source side only, the target-side tree is of great importance: the reordering rules can be only extracted if the words covered by the rule are entirely covered by both a node in the source and in the target trees. It allows the more accurate determination of the covering and limits of the extracted rules.

4.3 Rules organization

Once the list of fully lexicalized reordering patterns is extracted, all the rules are progressively processed reducing the amount of lexical information. These *initial rules* are iteratively expanded such that each element of the pattern is generalized until all the lexical elements of the rule are represented in the form of fully unlexicalized categories. Hence, from each

NN@0 NP@1 → NP@1 NN@0 | NN@0 << fndq >> NP@1 << +k >> | p
NN@0 NNP@1 → NNP@1 NN@0 | NN@0 << fndq >> NNP@1 << +k >> | p′

Figure 1: Directly extracted rules.

initial pattern with N lexical elements, $2^N - 2$ partially lexicalized rules and 1 general rule are generated. An example of the process of delexicalization can be found in Figure 3.

Thus, finally three types of rules are available: (1) fully lexicalized (initial) rules, (2) partially lexicalized rules and (3) unlexicalized (general) rules.

On the next step, the sets are processed separately: patterns are pruned and ambiguous rules are removed. All the rules from the fully lexicalized, partially lexicalized and general sets that appear fewer than k times are directly discarded (k is a shorthand for k_{ful}, k_{part} and k_{gener}). The probability of a pattern is estimated based on relative frequency of their appearance in the training corpus. Only one the most probable rule is stored. Fully lexicalized rules are not pruned ($k_{ful} = 0$); partially lexicalized rules that have been seen only once were discarded ($k_{part} = 1$); the thresholds k_{gener} was set to 3: it limits the number of general patterns capturing rare grammatical exceptions which can be easily found in any language.

Only the one-best reordering is used in other stages of the algorithm, so the rule output functioning as an input to the next rule can lead to situations reverting the change of word order that the previously applied rule made. Therefore, the rules that can be ambiguous when applied sequentially during decoding are pruned according to the higher probability principle. For example, for the pair of patterns with the same lexicon (which is empty for a general rule leading to a recurring contradiction *NP@0 VP@1* $\rightarrow$ *VP@1 NP@0 p1*, *VP@0 NP@1* $\rightarrow$ *NP@1 VP@0 p2*), the less probable rule is removed.

Finally, there are three resulting parameter tables analogous to the "r-table" as stated in (Yamada and Knight, 2001), consisting of POS- and constituent-based patterns allowing for reordering and monotone distortion (examples can be found in Table 5).

4.4 Source-side monotonization

Rule application is performed as a bottom-up parse tree traversal following two principles:

(1) the longest possible rule is applied, i.e. among a set of nested rules, the rule with a longest left-side covering is selected. For example, in the case of the appearance of an *NN JJ RB* sequence and presence of the two reordering rules

NN@0 JJ@1 $\rightarrow$ ... and

NN@0 JJ@1 RB@2 $\rightarrow$ ...

the latter pattern will be applied.

(2) the rule containing the maximum lexical information is applied, i.e. in case there is more than one alternative pattern from different groups, the lexicalized rules have preference over the partially lexicalized, and partially lexicalized over general ones.

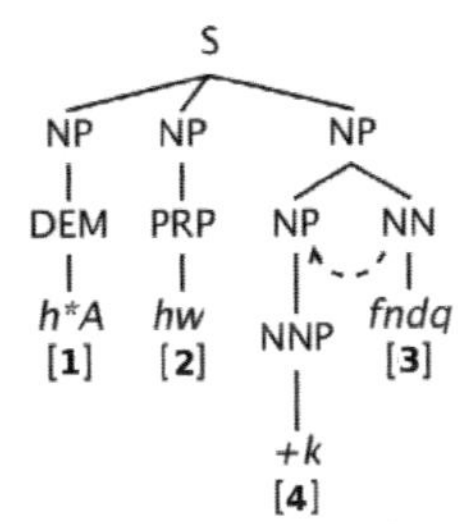

Figure 4: *Reordered source-side parse tree.*

Once the reordering of the training corpus is ready, it is realigned and new more monotonic alignment is passed to the SMT system. In theory, the word links from the original alignment can be used, however, due to our experience, running GIZA++ again results in a better word alignment since it is easier to learn on the modified training example.

Example of correct local reordering done with the SBR model can be found in Figure 4.

Initial rule: *NN@0 NP@1* $\rightarrow$ *NP@1 NN@0* | *NN@0* << *fndq* >> *NP@1* << *+k* >> | p_1

Part. lexic. rules: *NN@0 NP@1* $\rightarrow$ *NP@1 NN@0* | *NN@0* << *fndq* >> *NP@1* << - >> | p_2
NN@0 NP@1 $\rightarrow$ *NP@1 NN@0* | *NN@0* << - >> *NP@1* << *+k* >> | p_3

General rule: *NN@0 NP@1* $\rightarrow$ *NP@1 NN@0* | p_4

Figure 3: Example of a lexical rule expansion.

4.5 Coupling with decoding

In order to improve reordering power of the translation system, we implemented an additional reordering as described in Crego and Mariño (2006).

Multiple word segmentations is encoded in a lattice, which is then passed to the input of the decoder, containing reordering alternatives consistent with the previously extracted rules. The decoder takes the n-best reordering of a source sentence coded in the form of a word lattice. This approach is in line with recent research tendencies in SMT, as described for example in (Hildebrand et al., 2008; Xu et al., 2005). Originally, word lattice algorithms do not involve syntax into reordering process, therefore their reordering power is limited at representing long-distance reordering. Our approach is designed in the spirit of hybrid MT, integrating syntax transfer approach and statistical word lattice methods to achieve better MT performance on the basis of the standard state-of-the-art models.

During training a set of word permutation patterns is automatically learned following given word-to-word alignment. Since the original and monotonized (reordered) alignments may vary, different sets of reordering patterns are generated. Note that no information about the syntax of the sentence is used: the reordering permutations are motivated by the crossed links found in the word alignment and, con-

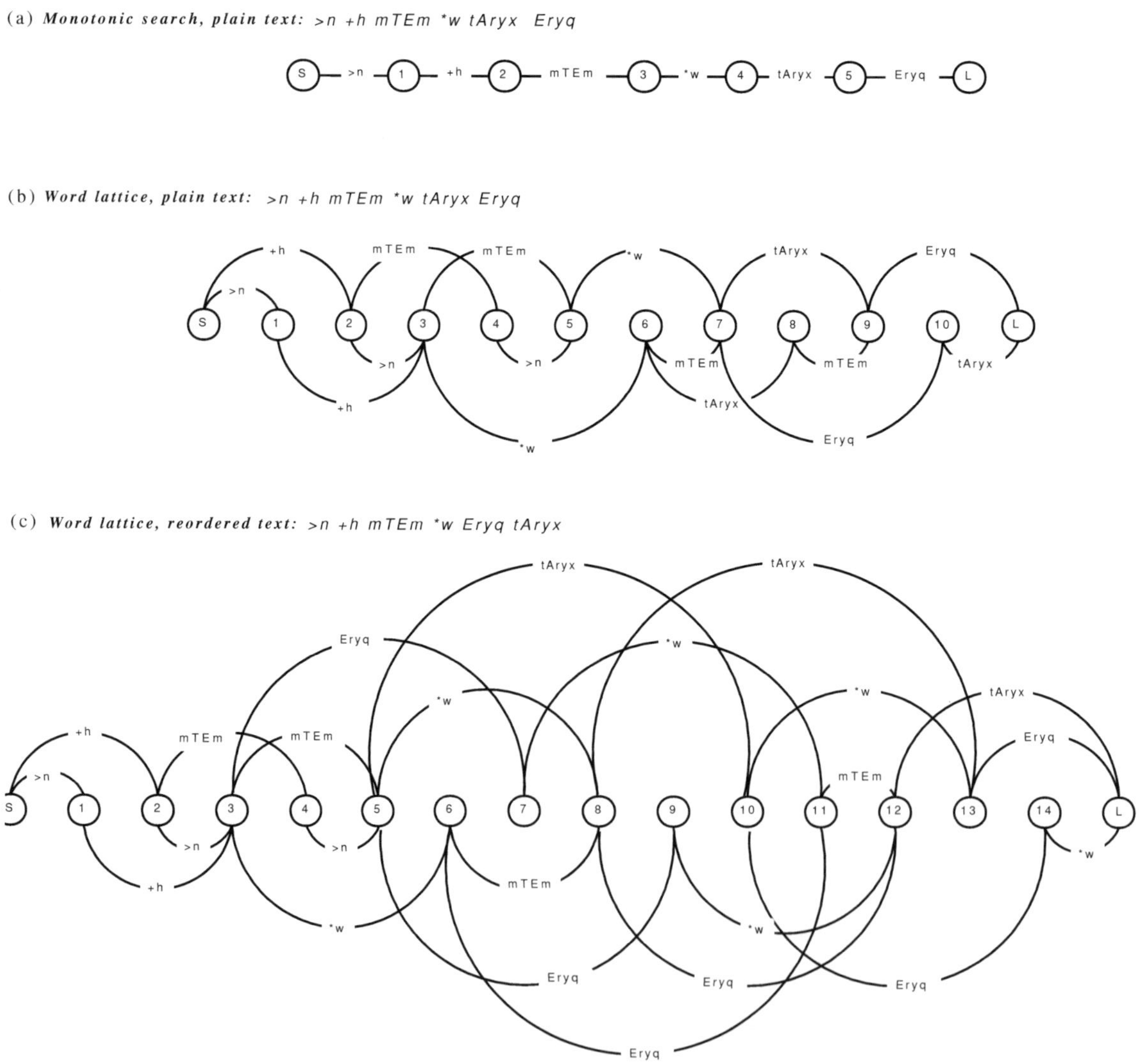

Figure 5: *Comparative example of a monotone search (a), word lattice for a plain (b) and reordered (c) source sentences.*

sequently, the generalization power of this framework is limited to local permutations.

On the step prior to decoding, the system generates word reordering graph for every source sentence, expressed in the form of a word lattice. The decoder processes word lattice instead of only one input hypothesis, extending the monotonic search graph with alternative paths.

Original sentence in Arabic, the English gloss and reference translation are:

Ar.:	*>n +h*	*mTEm*	**w*	*Eryq*	*tAryx*
Gl.:	this	restaurant	has	history	illustrious

Ref: 'this restaurant has an illustrious history'

The monotonic search graph (a) is extended with a word lattice for the monotonic train set (b) and reordered train sets (c). Figure 5 shows an example of the input word graph expressed in the form of a word lattice. Lattice (c) differ from the graph (b) in number of edges and provides more input options to the decoder. The decision about final translation is taken during decoding considering all the possible paths, provided by the word lattice.

5 Experiments and results

5.1 Data

The experiments were performed on two Arabic-English corpora: the BTEC'08 corpus from the tourist domain and the 50K first-lines extraction from the corpus that was provided to the NIST'08 evaluation campaign and belongs to the news domain (NIST50K). The corpora differ mainly in the average sentence length (ASL), which is the key corpus characteristic in global reordering studies.

A training set statistics can be found in Table 1.

	BTEC		NIST50K	
	Ar	En	Ar	En
Sentences	24.9 K	24.9 K	50 K	50 K
Words	225 K	210 K	1.2 M	1.35 M
ASL	9.05	8.46	24.61	26.92
Voc	11.4 K	7.6 K	55.3	36.3

Table 1: Basic statistics of the BTEC training corpus.

The BTEC development dataset consists of 489 sentences and 3.8 K running words, with 6 human-made reference translations per sentence; the dataset used to test the translation quality has 500 sentences, 4.1 K words and is also provided with 6 reference translations.

The NIST50K development set consists of 1353 sentences and 43 K words; the test data contains 1056 sentences and 33 K running words. Both datasets have 4 reference translations per sentence.

5.2 Arabic data preprocessing

We took a similar approach to that shown in Habash and Sadat (2006), using the MADA+TOKAN system for disambiguation and tokenization. For disambiguation only diacritic unigram statistics were employed. For tokenization we used the D3 scheme with -TAGBIES option. The scheme splits the following set of clitics: w+, f+, b+, k+, l+, Al+ and pronominal clitics. The -TAGBIES option produces Bies POS tags on all taggable tokens.

5.3 Experimental setup

We used the Stanford Parser (Klein and Manning, 2003) for both languages, Penn English Treebank (Marcus et al., 1993) and Penn Arabic Treebank set (Kulick et al., 2006). The English Treebank is provided with 48 POS and 14 syntactic tags, the Arabic Treebank has 26 POS and 23 syntactic categories.

As mentioned above, specific rules are not pruned away due to a limited amount of training material we set the thresholds k_{part} and k_{gener} to relatively low values, 1 and 3, respectively.

Evaluation conditions were case-insensitive and with punctuation marks considered. The target-side 4-gram language model was estimated using the SRILM toolkit (Stolcke, 2002) and modified Kneser-Ney discounting with interpolation. The highest BLEU score (Papineni et al., 2002) was chosen as the optimization criterion. Apart from BLEU, a standard automatic measure METEOR (Banerjee and Lavie, 2005) was used for evaluation.

5.4 Results

The scores considered are: BLEU scores obtained for the development set as the final point of the MERT procedure (*Dev*), and BLEU and METEOR scores obtained on test dataset (*Test*).

We present BTEC results (Tables 2), characterized by relatively short sentence length, and the results obtained on the NIST corpus (Tables 3) with much longer sentences and much need of global reordering.

	Dev	Test	
	BLEU	BLEU	METEOR
Plain	48.31	45.02	65.98
BL	48.46	47.10	68.10
SBR	48.75	47.52	67.33
SBR+lattice	48.90	48.78	68.85

Table 2: Summary of BTEC experimental results.

	Dev	Test	
	BLEU	BLEU	METEOR
Plain	41.83	43.80	62.03
BL	42.68	43.52	62.17
SBR	42.71	44.01	63.29
SBR+lattice	43.05	44.89	63.30

Table 3: Summary of NIST50K experimental results.

Four SMT systems are contrasted: *BL* refers to the Moses baseline system: the training data is not reordered, lexicalized reordering model (Tillman, 2004) is applied; *SBR* refers to the monotonic system configuration with reordered (SBR) source part; *SBR+lattice* is the run with reordered source part, on the translation step the input is represented as a word lattice.

We also compare the proposed approach with a monotonic system configuration (*Plain*). It shows the effect of source-reordering and lattice input, also decoded monotonically.

Automatic scores obtained on the test dataset evolve similarly when the SBR and word lattice representation applied to BTEC and NIST50K tasks. The combined method coupling two reordering techniques was more effective than the techniques applied independently and shows an improvement in terms of BLEU for both corpora. The METEOR score is only slightly better for the SBR configurations in case of BTEC task; in the case of NIST50K the METEOR improvement is more evident. The general trend is that automatic scores evaluated on the test set increase with the reordering model complexity.

Application of the SBR algorithm only (without a word lattice decoding) does not allow achieving statistical significance threshold for a 95% confidence interval and 1000 resamples (Koehn, 2004) for either of considered corpora. However, the *SBR+lattice* system configuration outperforms the *BL* by about 1.7 BLEU points (3.5%) for BTEC task and about 1.4 BLEU point (3.1%) for NIST task. These differences is statistically significant.

Figure 6 demonstrates how two reordering techniques interact within a sentence with a need for both global and local word permutations.

5.5 Syntax-based rewrite rules

As mentioned above, the SBR operates with three groups of reordering rules, which are the product of complete or partial delexicalization of the originally extracted patterns. The groups are processed and pruned independently. Basic rules statistics for both translation tasks can be found in Table 4.

The major part of reordering rules consists of two or three elements (for BTEC task there are no patterns including more than three nodes). For NIST50K there are a few rules with higher size in words of the move (up to 8). In addition, there are some long lexicalized rules (7-8), generating a high number of partially lexicalized patterns.

Table 5 shows the most frequent reordering rules with non-monotonic right part from each group.

Ar. plain.:	***AElnt***	*Ajhzp*	*AlAElAm*	*l*	*bEvp*	*AlAmm AlmtHdp*	*fy*	*syrAlywn*		*An*	...
En. gloss:	**announced**	press	release	by	mission	nations united	in	sierra	leone	that	...

En. ref.: 'a press release by the united nations mission to sierra leone **announced** that ...'

Ar. reord.: Ajhzp AlAElAm l bEvp AlmtHdp AlAmm fy syrAlywn ***AElnt*** *An ...*

Figure 6: Example of SBR application (**highlited bold**) and local reordering error corrected with word lattice reordering (underlined).

6 Conclusions

In this study we have shown how the translation quality can be improved, coupling (1) SBR algorithm and (2) word alignment-based reordering framework applied during decoding. The system automatically learns a set of syntactic reordering patterns that exploit systematic differences between word order of source and target languages.

Translation accuracy is clearly higher when allowing for SBR coupled with word lattice input representation than standard Moses SMT with existing (lexicalized) reordering models within the decoder and one input hypothesis condition. We have also compared the reordering model a monotonic system.

The method was tested translating from Arabic to English. Two corpora and tasks were considered: the BTEC task with much need of local reordering and the NIST50K task requiring long-distance permutations caused by longer sentences.

The reordering approach can be expanded for any other pair of languages with available parse tools. We also expect that the method scale to a large training set, and that the improvement will still be kept, however, we plan to confirm this assumption experimentally in the near future.

Acknowledgments

This work has been funded by the Spanish Government under grant TEC2006-13964-C03 (AVIVAVOZ project) and under a FPU grant.

Group	# of rules	Voc	2-element	3-element	4-element	[5-8]-element
BTEC experiments						
Specific rules	703	413	406	7	0	0
Partially lexicalized rules	1,306	432	382	50	0	0
General rules	259	5	259	0	0	0
NIST50K experiments						
Specific rules	517	399	193	109	72	25
Partially lexicalized rules	17,897	14,263	374	638	1,010	12,241
General rules	489	372	180	90	72	30

Table 4: Basic reordering rules statistics.

Specific rules

NN@0 NP@1 -> NP@1 NN@0 | NN@0 « Asm » NP@1 « +y » | 0.0270

DTNN@0 DTJJ@1 -> DTJJ@1 DTNN@0 | DTNN@0 « AlAmm »DTJJ@1 « AlmtHdp » | 0.0515

Partially lexicalized rules

DTNN@0 DTJJ@1 -> DTJJ@1 DTNN@0 | DTNN@0 « NON »DTJJ@1 « AlmtHdp » | 0.0017

NN@0 NNP@1 -> NNP@1 NN@0 | NN@0 « NON »NNP@1 « $rm » | 0.0017

General rules

PP@0 NP@1 -> PP@0 NP@1 | 0.0432

NN@0 DTNN@1 DTJJ@2 -> NN@0 DTJJ@2 DTNN@1 |0.0259

Table 5: Examples of Arabic-to-English reordering rules.

References

S. Banerjee and A. Lavie. 2005. METEOR: An automatic metric for MT evaluation with improved correlation with human judgments. In *Proceedings of the ACL Workshop on Intrinsic and Extrinsic Evaluation Measures for Machine Translation and/or Summarization*, pages 65–72.

M. Collins, Ph. Koehn, and I. Kučerová. 2005. Clause restructuring for statistical machine translation. In *Proceedings of the 43rd Annual Meeting on ACL 2005*, pages 531–540.

M.R. Costa-jussà and J.A.R. Fonollosa. 2006. Statistical machine reordering. In *Proceedings of the HLT/EMNLP 2006*.

M.R. Costa-jussà and J.A.R. Fonollosa. 2008. Computing multiple weighted reordering hypotheses for a statistical machine translation phrase-based system. In *In Proc. of the AMTA'08*, Honolulu, USA, October.

M.R. Costa-jussà, J.M. Crego, A. de Gispert, P. Lambert, M. Khalilov, J. A. Fonollosa, J.B. Mari no, and R.E. Banchs. 2006. TALP phrase-based system and TALP system combination for IWSLT 2006. In *Proceedings of the IWSLT 2006*, pages 123–129.

J.M. Crego and J. B Mariño. 2006. Reordering experiments for N-gram-based SMT. In *SLT'06*, pages 242–245.

J.M. Crego and J.B. Mariño. 2007. Syntax-enhanced N-gram-based smt. In *Proceedings of MT SUMMIT XI*.

J.M. Crego, J. B. Mariño, and A. de Gispert. 2005. Reordered search and tuple unfolding for ngram-based smt. In *In Proc. of MT SUMMIT X*, pages 283–289, September.

S. Nießen and H. Ney. 2004. Statistical machine translation with scarce resources using morpho-syntactic information. volume 30, pages 181–204.

N. Habash and F. Sadat. 2006. Arabic preprocessing schemes for statistical machine translation. In *Proceedings of the Human Language Technology Conference of the NAACL*, pages 49–52.

A.S. Hildebrand, K. Rottmann, M. Noamany, Q. Gao, S. Hewavitharana, N. Bach, and S. Vogel. 2008. Recent improvements in the cmu large scale chinese-english smt system. In *Proceedings of ACL-08: HLT (Companion Volume)*, pages 77–80.

K. Imamura, H. Okuma, and E. Sumita. 2005. Practical approach to syntax-based statistical machine translation. In *Proceedings of MT Summit X*, pages 267–274.

S. Kanthak, D. Vilar, E. Matusov, R. Zens, and H. Ney. 2005. Novel reordering approaches in phrase-based statistical machine translation. In *In Proc. of the ACL Workshop on Building and Using Parallel Texts*, pages 167–174, June.

D. Klein and C. Manning. 2003. Accurate unlexicalized parsing. In *Proceedings of the 41st Annual Meeting of the ACL 2003*, pages 423–430.

Ph. Koehn, F. J. Och, and D. Marcu. 2003. Statistical phrase-based machine translation. In *Proceedings of the HLT-NAACL 2003*, pages 48–54.

Ph. Koehn, H. Hoang, A. Birch, C. Callison-Burch, M. Federico, N. Bertoldi, B. Cowan, W. Shen, C. Moran, R. Zens, C. Dyer, O. Bojar, A. Constantin, and E. Herbst. 2007. Moses: open-source toolkit for statistical machine translation. In *Proceedings of ACL 2007*, pages 177–180.

Ph. Koehn. 2004. Statistical significance tests for machine translation evaluation. In *Proceedings of EMNLP 2004*, pages 388–395.

S. Kulick, R. Gabbard, and M. Marcus. 2006. Parsing the Arabic Treebank: Analysis and improvements. *Treebanks and Linguistic Theories*.

M.P. Marcus, B. Santorini, and M.A. Marcinkiewicz. 1993. Building a large annotated corpus of English: The Penn Treebank. *Computational Linguistics*, 19(2):313–330.

F. Och and H. Ney. 2003. A systematic comparison of various statistical alignment models. *Computational Linguistics*, 29(1):19–51.

F.J. Och, D. Gildea, S. Khudanpur, A. Sarkar, K. Yamada, A. Fraser, S. Kumar, L. Shen, D. Smith, K. Eng, V. Jain, Z. Jin, and D. Radev. 2004. A Smorgasbord of Features for Statistical Machine Translation. In *Proceedings of HLT/NAACL04*, pages 161–168.

K. Papineni, S. Roukos, T. Ward, and W. Zhu. 2002. Bleu: a method for automatic evaluation of machine translation. In *Proceedings of ACL 2002*, pages 311–318.

A. Stolcke. 2002. SRILM: an extensible language modeling toolkit. In *Proceedings of the Int. Conf. on Spoken Language Processing*, pages 901–904.

C. Tillman. 2004. A unigram orientation model for statistical machine translation. In *Proceedings of HLT-NAACL'04*.

C. Wang, M. Collins, and P. Koehn. 2007. Chinese syntactic reordering for statistical machine translation. In *Proceedings of the Joint Conference on EMNLP*.

F. Xia and M. McCord. 2004. Improving a statistical mt system with automatically learned rewrite patterns. In *Proceedings of the COLING 2004*.

J. Xu, E. Matusov, R. Zens, and H. Ney. 2005. Integrated chinese word segmentation in statistical machine translation. In *Proc. of IWSLT 2005*.

K. Yamada and K. Knight. 2001. A syntax-based statistical translation model. In *Proceedings of ACL 2001*, pages 523–530.

Author Index